# ADVANCE PRAISE FOR CONNECTION CULTURE

"*Connection Culture* lays out a compelling case for a culture of connection in every organization, and provides a framework for leaders who want to apply positive personal values in practice in their organizations and teams."

—John Young
Group President, Global Established Pharma Businesses, Pfizer

"Engaging, while offering real solutions to human challenges that occur in the workplace! As someone who has researched and published in the field of organizational psychology, I can honestly say that *Connection Culture* is right on target and a book that every leader should race to get his or her hands on."

—Karla R. Peters-Van Havel
Chief Operating Officer, The Institute for Management Studies

"Listening to and engaging staffers in the right way at all levels is the key to driving business forward and is at the heart of Michael's book. Running an organization of some 8,000 people, I have found Michael's experience, guidance, and philosophy helpful in understanding and improving our company's performance on multiple metrics. I hope others find the inspiration in this book that has helped FCB be better at what we do."

—Carter Murray
Worldwide CEO, Foote, Cone & Belding

"*Connection Culture* offers a wealth of information, insights, and counsel that can help any organization develop a connection culture."

—Robert Morris
Business Book Reviewer, BobMorris.biz and Amazon.com

"*Connection Culture* grabbed my attention from the beginning and had me jumping on the phone to share its ideas with friends and colleagues. We have to do better as leaders and as teachers of leadership development to be intentional in creating and sustaining connection cultures. Even when you think you've got it all in place (the surveys, training, recognition awards, and celebrations), disconnection creeps in. You must read this book."

—Janis Apted
Associate Vice President, Faculty and Academic Development
The University of Texas MD Anderson Cancer Center

"Much has been written about the impact of culture on organizational performance. *Connection Culture* digs deeper, putting the spotlight on the fundamental role that emotional connections play in fueling engagement, collaboration, and productivity. The ideas set out in this book will help you bring your people together to focus on collective success that results in a significant shift in your organization's performance."

—Bryan Crawford
Global Vice Chairman, Foote Cone & Belding

"Our organization has benefited greatly from the principles in *Connection Culture*. The book creates an engaging framework for leaders who want more for their businesses and employees. It is a must read for anyone leading an organization."

—Mike Cunnion
Chief Executive Officer, Remedy Health Media

"Once again Michael Lee Stallard has mastered a rich description of the connection culture. He narrates a very concise and powerful road map to guide you as a leader and manager. Want to get strong results and fully develop your colleagues? Stallard's ideas are compelling and abundant, providing practical actions to develop and refine your connection culture. Don't wait another moment. Get a copy for yourself. And for your colleagues. They will thank you."

—Tom Jansen
Team Leader, Strategy, Strategic Performance Office,
Boy Scouts of America

"Too many leadership books focus on developing work experience without acknowledging the rest of our lives. *Connection Culture* demonstrates how the positive habits, relationships, and character we've developed in the workplace can serve us well at home and in our communities. Not only does this deep exploration of connection culture explain the positive effects of using these skills, it also offers ways to get started on the journey."

—James DaSilva
Senior Editor, *SmartBrief on Leadership*

"Thank you, Michael, for reminding us again that people—customers and employees—are the most important ingredient of any business. Leaders place so much emphasis on the operations and financials, but people connecting and working together is the key to success."

—Jay Morris
Vice President, Leadership Development and Education
Executive Director, Institute for Excellence
Yale New Haven Health System

"The message of Connection Culture is profoundly personal yet ultimately universal. If you think you know what connection really means, you'll come away with a whole new perspective after reading this gracefully written book."

—Bruce Rosenstein
Managing Editor, *Leader to Leader*
Author, *Create Your Future the Peter Drucker Way*

"Connection Culture has everything you need in a leadership book: it inspires, it's backed by solid research, and it has practical, proven ideas and action steps. If you are looking for ways to motivate, engage, foster innovation, or perhaps simply striving for a richer life for yourself and others, read and re-read Connection Culture."

—Dan McCarthy
Leadership author, consultant, and executive coach

"Connection works when we work on connection. Michael Stallard draws us in with his stories, convinces us with his evidence, and guides us with his recommendations. He concludes by inviting us to mark the day we finish the book as the start of a new outlook, focused on establishing a thriving work culture through freshly enlivened, engaged, and enriched connections."

—David Zinger
Employee Engagement Global Expert
Founder, Employee Engagement Network

# MICHAEL LEE STALLARD

WITH JASON PANKAU AND KATHARINE P. STALLARD

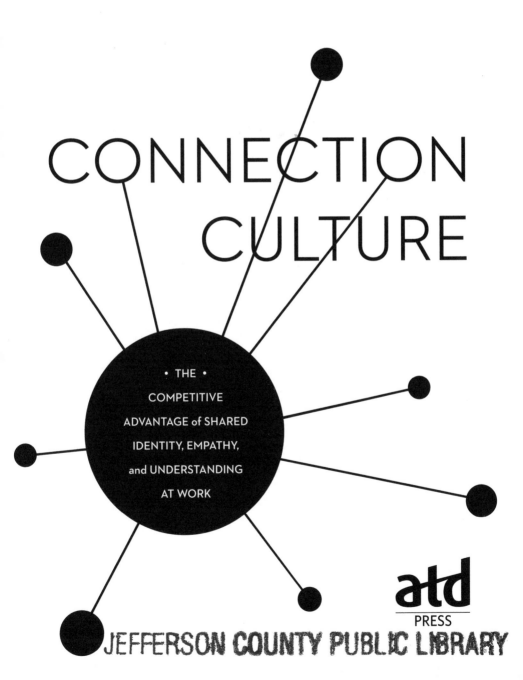

# CONNECTION CULTURE

• THE •
COMPETITIVE
ADVANTAGE of SHARED
IDENTITY, EMPATHY,
and UNDERSTANDING
AT WORK

**atd**
PRESS

Parts of this book are adapted from articles in *Leader to Leader* from the Frances
Hesselbein Leadership Institute.

The Via Institute Classification of Character Strengths is copyright 2004-2014, VIA
Institute on Character. All rights reserved. www.viacharacter.org.

**ATD Press** is an internationally renowned source of insightful and practical information
on talent development, workplace learning, and professional development.

ATD Press
1640 King Street
Alexandria, VA 22314 USA

658.314
STA

Ordering information: Books published by ATD Press can be purchased by visiting
ATD's website at www.td.org/books or by calling 800.628.2783 or 703.683.8100.

Library of Congress Control Number: 2015932216

ISBN-10: 1-56286-927-2
ISBN-13: 978-1-56286-927-4
e-ISBN: 978-1-60728-499-4

**ATD Press Editorial Staff**
Director: Kristine Luecker
Manager: Christian Green
Community of Practice Manager, Management: Ron Lippock
Associate Editor: Melissa Jones
Cover Design: Emily Weigel, Faceout Studio
Text Design: Lon Levy, Marisa Fritz, and Maggie Hyde
Printed by Maple Press, York, PA, www.MaplePress.com

# CONTENTS

# FOREWORD
## BY VICTOR J. BOSCHINI JR.

*Connection Culture* presents a new way of thinking about leadership, employee engagement, and organizational health. It shares the stories of many different organizations that found tremendous success by nurturing connections—from Pixar to the U.S. Navy to the Duke University men's basketball team. Combined with an array of data and research findings, as well as examples from real-life experiences, Michael Lee Stallard makes the compelling case that a culture of connection provides a clear competitive advantage for organizations and individuals. *Connection Culture* provides powerful tools for enriching and transforming organizations, continuing and deepening the conversation begun in Stallard's highly acclaimed book *Fired Up or Burned Out*.

Texas Christian University is proud to be one of the organizations profiled in *Connection Culture*. At TCU our goal is to produce graduates who can deal with change and ambiguity, assess risk, and motivate others. These are the qualities most needed for leadership in an unpredictable environment. This emphasis on the individual also extends to faculty and staff—the Chronicle of Higher Education continually recognizes TCU as one of the 100 Great Colleges to Work For.

But we want to do more.

Some years ago I was intrigued to learn that Stallard, the father of two of our students, was an expert on leadership and organizational culture. When I read what he wrote on connection culture it really resonated with me. During the course of my career in higher education, I've seen how students thrive when supportive relationships make them feel connected, and I've seen how they struggle when they feel lonely. I was thankful to see how well TCU resonated with Stallard's connection culture theory—the university's culture is rooted in a long history of valuing service to others and inclusiveness, both of which increase connection.

In an effort to strengthen our culture of connection even further, TCU is partnering with Stallard to create a Center for Connection Culture at the university. Through the leadership of Chancellor's Associate for Strategic Partnerships Ann Louden, who is also the Center's director, we are committed to embracing connection cultures in higher education. It begins at home as we equip our faculty, staff, and students with the skills to be more intentional about connection. Our strong connection culture on campus is being enhanced by the work of the Center. And we are committed to embracing connection programs and activities for our entire university, as well as for community participants.

While reading *Connection Culture*, I was reminded of Moore's Law, which states that the processing power of computers will double every two years. I find this to be an apt metaphor for the rapidly evolving environment we must prepare our TCU graduates for. This book provides positive ways of thinking and acting that can help them—and us all—navigate that unpredictable future.

—Victor J. Boschini Jr.
Chancellor
Texas Christian University

# FOREWORD
## BY TED GEORGE

As a practicing psychiatrist and neuroscience researcher, I've seen how important work is in people's lives, as well as the impact it can have on their emotional well-being. As I talk with people, I often hear about their problems with supervisors, boredom with work, or being overwhelmed with responsibilities. These situations and others like them have a negative impact on job performance and mental health.

Steps need to be taken to change the status quo. Michael Lee Stallard's *Connection Culture* not only ventures into research about the positive influence a connection can have on the work environment, it also offers practical approaches to make a change. Such tools have tremendously positive implications for managers and employees, as well as the companies that count on superior performance to stay competitive.

In the book, Stallard focuses on the six universal needs humans have to thrive: respect, recognition, belonging, autonomy, personal growth, and meaning. When these needs are not met, the nervous system responds with anger, fear, or a passive state of "disconnect" in order to restore a sense of well-being. In a healthy workplace, these emotions serve to right wrongs and re-establish a thriving environment where the autonomic nervous system and endocrine system promote a sense of well-being and good health. However, when interactions and the general office environment don't meet those six needs, they can cause unhealthy emotional responses by both employees and managers. These feelings of disconnection make people more vulnerable to stress, anxiety, depression, and addiction.

Only recently has modern technology allowed us to understand the profound effect that feelings of exclusion have on the nervous system.

A group of scientists at the University of California placed participants in an fMRI scanner and examined how the blood flow in their brains changed when they were excluded from social interaction. One interesting observation was that in some of the individuals the rejection activated the part of the brain that processes pain. *Connection Culture* builds on these ideas, highlighting findings from other researchers to champion the importance of connection within the workplace. This research demonstrates how increasing connection has a favorable effect on organizational outcomes, including higher customer satisfaction, revenue, and profits, and lower employee turnover and accident rates.

Stallard also includes many case studies featuring organizations and managers that have excelled at creating a culture that connects people. These stories provide real-life examples of leaders who had the courage and insight to take a dysfunctional organization and inspire change by empowering people to truly succeed and have a sense of importance and meaning. Stallard uses them to demonstrate how connection culture provides a competitive advantage in a variety of fields, including business, government, healthcare, higher education, and sports, as well as the religious and social sectors.

In addition to telling the stories of successful leaders, *Connection Culture* also offers a wealth of practical advice. It provides 15 building blocks to help leaders get started—five each in vision, value, and voice. These encouraging, helpful suggestions are easy and approachable, and will set you on the path to connecting people.

The book ends with the message that connection begins with you. In my psychiatric practice I see many people get to the point of change, but then get bogged down with pessimistic thoughts, such as "it won't work" or "no one will listen to me." *Connection Culture* asks you to take an honest look at yourself as an employee, a manager, and a leader, and to take ownership of the culture. The rewards you reap will not only empower you, but also your employees. It will give you the satisfaction of knowing that you are helping to make your organization a healthier and better place to work.

—Ted George, MD
Clinical Professor at George Washington School of Medicine
Senior Investigator at The National Institute on Alcohol
Abuse and Alcoholism
Author of *Untangling the Mind: Why We Behave the Way We Do*

# INTRODUCTION
## THE SECRET
## OF U2'S SUCCESS

U2 began as a rock band that people booed and laughed at. Now, after receiving its 22nd Grammy Award in 2005, U2 has more than any band in history. It recently surpassed the Rolling Stones's record for the highest revenue grossing concert tour ever. Critics rave over the band's music, and fans worldwide can't seem to get enough of its songs and concert appearances. All the signs indicate that U2 is at the top of its game and will be going strong for the foreseeable future. So how did this group rise to such lofty heights, and what can we learn from its success?

The way U2 functions is even more extraordinary than its music. The band's four members—lyricist and lead singer Bono, lead guitar player "the Edge," bass guitar player Adam Clayton, and drummer Larry Mullen Jr.—have known one another since they were teenagers in Dublin, Ireland. Bono has described the band as more of an organism than an organization, and several of its attributes contribute to this unique culture. Members value continuous improvement to achieve their own potential, always maintaining the view that they can become even better.

U2's members share a vision of their mission and values. You might expect a band's mission to be achieving commercial success as measured by number 1 hits and concert attendance. However, U2's mission is to improve the world through its music and influence. Bono has described himself as a traveling salesman of ideas within songs, which address themes the band members believe are important to promote, including human rights, social justice, and matters of faith. Bono and his wife, Ali, help the poor, particularly in Africa, through their philanthropy and the organizations they've created.

U2's members value one another as people and don't just think of one another as means to an end. Bono has said that although he hears melodies in his head, he is unable to translate them into written music. Considering himself a terrible guitar and keyboard player, he relies on his fellow members to help him write the songs and praises them for their talents, which are integral to U2's success.

Bono has also had his band members' backs during times of trial. When Larry lost his mom in a car accident a short time after the band was formed, Bono was there to support him. Bono, who had already lost his mother, understood Larry's pain. When U2 was offered its first recording contract on the condition that it replace Larry with a more conventional drummer, Bono told the record company executive: There's no deal without Larry. When the Edge went through divorce, his bandmates were there to support him. When Adam showed up to a concert so stoned he couldn't perform, the others could have thrown him overboard for letting them down. Instead, they had someone step in to cover for him, and then went on to help Adam overcome his drug and alcohol addiction.

Bono's bandmates have his back too. One of the most vivid examples of this came when U2 campaigned during the 1980s for the observance of a Martin Luther King Jr. Day in the United States. Bono received a death threat that warned him not to sing "Pride (In the Name of Love)," a song about the Rev. Martin Luther King Jr., at an upcoming concert. The FBI considered it a credible threat. Bono described in an interview that as he sang the song, he closed his eyes. When he opened his eyes again at the end of a verse, he discovered that Adam was standing in front of him to shield him from potential harm. Years later, when U2 was inducted into the Rock and Roll Hall of Fame, Bono thanked Adam for being willing to take a bullet for him.

Unlike many bands in which one megastar gets most of the economic profits, U2 shares its profits equally among the four band members and their long-time manager. This further shows the value Bono has for his band members and manager. (We're not saying that all organizations should split the company's economic profits equally; simply recognize that when leaders take too much it works against engaging the people they lead.)

Each member has a voice in decisions, thanks to the band's participatory, consensus-oriented decision-making approach. If one person strongly opposes a particular action, the band won't do it, which encourages the flow of knowledge among band members, allowing the best ideas to come to light. Their passion for excellence is also reflected in relentless arguments over their music. Bono has stated that this approach can be slow and frustrating at times, but the members of U2 believe it is necessary to achieve excellence.

These factors—which this book calls shared identity, empathy, and understanding—create a culture of connection, community, and unity among the members of U2. Bono has described the band as a tight-knit family and community. Their commitment to support one another extends beyond the four members of the band to a larger community that includes their families, crew members, and collaborators—many of whom have known each other for decades.

The secret of U2's success is its leadership and culture. Bono connects as a leader among equals because he communicates an inspiring vision and lives it, he values people as individuals, and he gives them a voice in decision making. It is this culture of vision, value, and voice that has helped U2 achieve and sustain its superior performance.

This is a connection culture. In examining how U2 operates we see the influence a connection culture can have on the individual, as well as the group as a whole.

## HOW ABOUT YOU?

An organization's culture reflects the predominant ways of thinking, behaving, and working. To appreciate the importance of culture in the workplace, consider your own experiences. During the course of your career, have you experienced times when you were eager to get to work in the morning, you were so immersed in your work that the hours flew by, and by the end of the day you didn't want to stop working? What was it about the job that made you feel that way?

How about the opposite? Have you experienced times when you struggled to get to work in the morning, the hours passed ever so slowly, and by the end of the day you were exhausted? Again, what was it about the job that made you feel that way?

If you are like most people, you've experienced those extremes during your career. I have too. As I reflected on my experiences, I realized I hadn't changed—the culture I was in was either energizing or draining the life out of me.

Thus I began a quest to identify the elements of workplace cultures that help people and organizations thrive for sustained periods of time. When the practices my team and I developed to boost employee engagement contributed to doubling our business's revenues during the course of two and a half years, I knew I was on to something. A few years later I left Wall Street to devote my full attention to understanding employee engagement and culture so I could help others improve the cultures they were in.

# THREE PSYCHOSOCIAL CULTURES: CONNECTION, CONTROL, INDIFFERENCE

What type of culture are you in right now? As we explore what it takes to establish and strengthen connection cultures, it is instructive to understand how they differ from cultures of control and cultures of indifference.

In cultures of control, people with power, influence, and status rule over others. This culture creates an environment where people fear to make mistakes and take risks. It is stifling—killing innovation because people are afraid to speak up. Employees may feel left out, micromanaged, unsafe, hyper-criticized, or helpless.

Cultures of indifference are predominant today. In this type of culture, people are so busy chasing money, power, and status that they fail to invest the time necessary to develop healthy, supportive relationships. As a result, leaders don't see value in the relational nature of work, and many people struggle with loneliness. Employees may feel like a cog in a machine, unimportant, uncertain, or invisible.

Both of these cultures sabotage individual and organizational performance. Feeling consistently unsupported, left out, or lonely takes a toll. Without the psychological resources to cope with the normal stress of modern organizational life, employees may turn to unhealthy attitudes and behaviors, many of which are addictive and destructive.

A distinguishing feature of these cultures is a sole focus on task excellence. Leaders may openly dismiss the need for relationship excellence. Others may give it lip service and occasional attention, or see its value without knowing how to bring it about. In order to achieve sustainable, superior performance, every member of an organization needs to intentionally develop *both* task excellence and relationship excellence. A connection culture produces relationship excellence.

In a connection culture people care about others and care about their work because it benefits other human beings. They invest the time to develop healthy relationships and reach out to help others in need, rather than being indifferent to them. This bond helps overcome the differences that historically divided people, creating a sense of connection, community, and unity that is inclusive and energized, and spurs productivity and innovation.

## A MAJOR OPPORTUNITY FOR YOU

Understanding the factors that create a connection culture that enables us to thrive is extremely important. According to Gallup's employee engagement research during the last decade, 70 to 74 percent of American workers are not engaged in their jobs. Globally, that percentage rises to 87 to 89 percent (Gallup 2013). Disengaged people show up for the paycheck, but don't perform anywhere near what they are capable of if they were in a culture that energized and engaged them.

This lack of employee engagement is a problem that has serious ramifications. The business world is becoming a much more global and competitive place, with standards going up all the time. Organizations with a large percentage of disengaged employees may not survive. Individuals who fall behind thanks to poor work cultures will also be in trouble.

This may sound bleak, but you should consider it to be a major opportunity. In *Connection Culture* you will gain the knowledge to become part of the turnaround story and create cultures that help people thrive, whether you are a leader in a formal position of management or leadership authority, or if you informally lead others through your influence as a concerned employee who wants to see change. It will give you the tools to become more intentional about putting yourself in a healthy culture; creating a culture to boost employee engagement, productivity, innovation, and performance; and implementing actions that increase and sustain the health of the culture you work in. Although *Connection Culture* is focused on organizations and the workplace, it also applies to the culture in your family, volunteer group, and community.

In chapters 1 and 2 you will learn about the force of connection, the six universal human needs required to thrive at work, and the five elements that are necessary to create connection cultures that achieve sustainable superior performance.

Chapter 3 demonstrates in practical terms how connection applies to all groups through inspiring stories about the connection cultures of diverse organizations. You will learn how leaders and organizations in many different sectors incorporate connection.

Chapter 4 arms you with interesting and relevant research supporting the case for connection from a wide variety of fields, including psychology, sociology, neuroscience, and organizational behavior. You will also see how a lack of connection affects a person's wellness, well-being, and length of life.

Chapters 5 and 6 equip you with very specific, practical, and actionable ways to create a connection culture. In these final chapters you will discover ways to connect—including new ways to think about your attitudes, language, and behaviors.

*Connection Culture* provides a new way of thinking about leadership and organizational culture. In the pages ahead you will learn about this new approach and discover how to tap into the power of human connection.

# 1

# THE COMPETITIVE ADVANTAGE OF CONNECTION

---

In this chapter you will learn:

- the definition of connection and its effect on organizations and individuals

- the six universal human needs to thrive at work.

---

One of the most powerful and least understood aspects of successful organizations is how employees' feelings of connection, community, and unity provide a competitive advantage. Employees in an organization with a high degree of connection are more engaged, more productive in their jobs, and less likely to leave for a competitor. They are also more trusting and cooperative; they are more willing to share information with their colleagues and therefore help them make well-informed decisions.

Connection in the workplace is an emotional bond that promotes trust, cooperation, and esprit de corps among people. It is based on a shared identity, empathy, and understanding that moves primarily *self*-centered individuals toward *group*-centered membership. Without that sense of connection, employees will never reach their potential as individuals. And if employees don't reach their potential, the organization won't either. Connection is what transforms a dog-eat-dog environment into a sled dog team that pulls together.

When interacting with people, we generally find a connection with some, but not with others—"we really connected" and "we just didn't connect" are common phrases in our daily conversations. Connection describes something intangible that we sense in relationships. When it is present, we feel energy, empathy, and affirmation, and are more open; when it is absent, we experience neutral or even negative feelings.

Although we know what it's like to feel connected on a personal level, few understand the effect connection has on us, our families and friends, and our co-workers and the organizations we work in. Let me explain the power of connection by sharing some observations from my personal experiences.

I left Wall Street in May 2002 to begin researching and writing the book *Fired Up or Burned Out: How to Reignite Your Team's Passion, Creativity, and Productivity*. In addition to researching organizational behavior, psychology, sociology, history, political science, and systems theory, I did a great deal of reflecting about my own life experiences. To my surprise, some of the things I learned came from unexpected places.

## EPIPHANY

In late 2002, my wife, Katie, was diagnosed with breast cancer. During her treatments, we were comforted by the kindness and compassion of healthcare workers at our local hospital, some of whom were cancer survivors themselves. The connection we felt with them boosted our spirits.

Twelve months later, tests indicated that Katie might have ovarian cancer. January 7, 2004, was one of the most sobering days of my life—after her three-hour surgery, we found out that it was ovarian cancer, and that it had spread. I still remember the surgeon telling me that he was sorry. That night I took our daughters (Sarah, 12, and

Elizabeth, 10) and Katie's mom to visit her in the ICU. Seeing her so weak and pale scared the girls. Sarah backed up against a wall and began to faint. After an ICU nurse helped us revive her, we knew it was time to head home. As we walked through the deserted hospital lobby, Elizabeth began to sob. Sarah and I wrapped our arms around Elizabeth until she regained her composure. I recall how alone I felt and afraid of what the future might hold for our family.

After six chemotherapy treatments and a short break, Katie started a second regimen of chemotherapy, this time at Memorial Sloan Kettering Cancer Center in New York City. On our first visit, as we got within eyesight of the 53rd Street entrance in midtown Manhattan, a larger-than-life friendly doorman named Nick Medley locked eyes with Katie and smiled at her. This was the first of many happy surprises—few make eye contact with a passerby in New York City, let alone smile! I realized that Nick was probably a seasoned wig-spotter and, recognizing that Katie was a cancer patient, was intentionally reaching out to connect with her. In the lobby, the receptionist called everyone "honey." (Again, very unlike Manhattan.) Each person we encountered was friendly. Katie's oncologist, Dr. Martee Hensley, spent an hour educating us about treatment options and answering our long list of questions. Her warmth and optimistic attitude gave us hope.

By the end of the visit, I had two reactions. First, I had done the research and knew this was one of the best teams in the world to treat ovarian cancer. That was a rational reaction. Second, I believed that they cared. Even though I knew Katie's chance of survival was less than 10 percent, I was hopeful that these amazing people would get her through the difficult season ahead.

One day while Katie was undergoing treatment I stumbled upon a meeting in a lounge where employees who worked at that location were discussing the results of an employee survey. Nick was there and

I overheard him say that he loved working at the center because he loved his colleagues, the patients, and their families—and most of all he loved the cause, which is to provide "the best cancer care, anywhere." It was apparent that Nick's co-workers also felt a connection with one another, their patients, and their patients' families. During the time we spent at Sloan Kettering it struck me how much more joy and esprit de corps I felt in a cancer treatment center than I experienced while working on Wall Street. I wasn't at all surprised when I saw a segment about Nick on ABC's *World News Tonight* that said that this cancer survivor gives 1,300 hugs a day to patients and their families.

According to the American Cancer Society one of the worst things for cancer patients is to feel alone. We rarely felt alone. I'm convinced that the connections we felt with healthcare workers, friends, and family helped Katie go into remission and protected our family's spirits. When people stopped by to visit us, which happened regularly, it wasn't a somber occasion—we talked, laughed, and enjoyed one another's company. Christian, Jewish, and Muslim friends told us they were praying for Katie and our family, and an atheist friend said he was sending positive thoughts our way.

Having had such a good experience at Memorial Sloan Kettering Cancer Center, we enthusiastically recommended it to a friend of ours who was diagnosed with a different type of cancer. The physicians in that specialty were located in a different building, and surprisingly, her experience was completely at odds with ours. After the initial consultation, she felt alone and unwelcome and decided to seek treatment elsewhere.

Reflecting on these experiences made me realize three things about connection:

1. It is a powerful force that creates a positive emotional bond between people.

2. It contributes to bringing out the best in people and energizes them, making them more trusting and more resilient to face life's inevitable difficulties.

3. It can vary dramatically across teams, units, and even locations of organizations, depending upon local culture and leadership.

In 2014, Katie was diagnosed with another episode of breast cancer. When we returned to Memorial Sloan Kettering Cancer Center we found that the connection was just as strong as ever. Katie's surgeon, Dr. Alexandra Heerdt, her oncologist, Dr. Tiffany Traina, and their teams were upbeat and optimistic. On the day of Katie's surgery we arrived at the hospital at 7 a.m. and found Dr. Heerdt dressed in hospital scrubs waiting for us in the reception area. She gave Katie a big hug and asked if we had any questions. After the surgery Dr. Heerdt told me that she had removed the tumor and it appeared that it hadn't spread (which was later confirmed by lab results). When we met with Dr. Traina later to discuss adjuvant treatment options, she was personable and compassionate. With our faith and the power of connection, we are optimistic Katie will overcome this cancer too.

## BACKED BY SCIENCE

As I continued my research it was exciting to see hard evidence corroborate what I was seeing anecdotally. Neuroscientists and endocrinologists have discovered that human connection reduces the levels of the stress hormones epinephrine, norepinephrine, and cortisol in the blood so we are more likely to make rational decisions; triggers the release of an enzyme named telomerase, which heals damage to the telomeres on the tips of our chromosomes caused by stress; increases the neurotransmitter dopamine, which enhances attention and pleasure; increases serotonin, which reduces fear and worry; and increases the levels of oxytocin and/or vasopressin, which makes us more trusting of others (Hallowell 1999; Sapolsky 2008).

Other research establishes that connection improves wellness, well-being, and performance throughout our lifetime, indicating that we are biochemically hardwired for connection. It enhances the quality and length of our lives. Conversely, disconnection (social isolation or exclusion) brings about dysfunction and depression.

This is also supported by the observations of psychiatrists. For example, Edward Hallowell, a practicing psychiatrist and former instructor of psychiatry at Harvard Medical School, has written that most of the business executives he encounters in his practice are deprived of connection. They report loneliness, isolation, confusion, distrust, disrespect, and dissatisfaction, so Hallowell helps them identify ways to increase connection in their lives (Hallowell 1999b).

## HUMAN BEINGS, NOT MACHINES

Why is connection so powerful? Because humans are not machines—we have emotions, hopes and dreams, and a conscience.

Humans also have universal needs that must be met in order to thrive. It's important to understand that these are *needs* not just *wants* (or desires). The resulting sense of connection from having these needs met makes us feel connected to our work, the people we work with, and our organization. The work context has six specific needs: respect, recognition, belonging, autonomy, personal growth, and meaning. This list is derived from personal research, as well as research and insights from A.H. Maslow on the hierarchy of needs and need deficits, Mihaly Csikszentmihalyi on flow and optimal experience, Richard M. Ryan and Edward L. Deci on autonomy, and Viktor E. Frankl on meaning.

The first three needs (respect, recognition, and belonging) are *relational* needs. When these are met, we feel connected to the people we work with. The next two (autonomy and personal growth) are *task mastery* needs, which affect how connected we feel to the work we are doing. Finally, the sixth need, meaning, is an *existential* need.

## RESPECT

We need to be around people who are courteous and considerate. People who are patronizing, condescending, or passive-aggressive drain the life out of us and keep us from thriving.

## RECOGNITION

We get energized when we work with people who recognize and voice our task strengths, "you're a great manager," or character strengths, "you persevere to overcome obstacles." It's almost as if we have a recognition battery that periodically needs to be recharged—except that the outlet is on our back, where we can't reach, so we have to rely on those around us to charge our battery. If it's not charged, we feel emotionally and physically drained.

## BELONGING

When we feel as though we belong to a group, we are more resilient to cope with life's inevitable difficulties. And don't worry, *everyone* has them—sickness, death, job loss, divorce, depression, and so on are part of life. The people in our group help us through hard times because they care. (And they also tell us when we have food on our chin or are doing something unwise.) They care enough to tell us what we need to hear and are there for us when we need them.

## AUTONOMY

We need the freedom to do our work. Being micromanaged or slowed down by red tape, bureaucracy, or control-obsessed personalities prevents us from thriving.

## PERSONAL GROWTH

When we are engaged in a task that is a good fit with our strengths and provides the right degree of challenge, we experience a state that psychologists describe as flow. It is like being in a time warp—time flies by when we are immersed in a task. Unchallenged, we feel bored.

Over-challenged, we feel stressed out. The optimal degree of challenge invigorates us.

## MEANING

When we are engaged in work that is important to us in some way, we are energized and put additional effort into it. When our work has meaning, we feel a sense of significance.

# CONNECTION IS CRITICAL TO ORGANIZATIONS

It follows that the effect of connection on individual performance will have an influence on an organizational level. There is an extensive amount of research showing that connection provides a competitive advantage, which we'll review in greater detail in chapter 4. For now, consider this:

- Compared to business units with engagement and connection scores in the bottom 25 percent, the top 25 percent's median averages were:
    - 21 percent higher in productivity
    - 22 percent higher in profitability
    - 41 percent lower in quality defects
    - 37 percent lower in absenteeism
    - 10 percent higher in customer metrics (Gallup 2013).
- Employees who feel engaged and connected are:
    - 20 percent more productive than the average employee
    - 87 percent less likely to leave the organization (Corporate Leadership Council 2004).

Fostering connection in the workplace is a win-win for individuals and for organizations. Given the evidence, it is irrational not to be intentional about connection because it is the key to help you thrive personally and professionally. It affects the health of your family, workplace, volunteer organizations, community, and nation. You cannot thrive for long without it.

The following chapters demonstrate how you can bring out connection in the workplace by creating a connection culture—a culture with the necessary elements to meet our human needs.

# 2

# SHARED IDENTITY, EMPATHY, AND UNDERSTANDING

---

In this chapter you will learn:

- the three elements that contribute to connection

- the 24 character strengths necessary for building a connection culture

- the roles that committed members and servant leaders play in shaping an organization's culture.

---

People occasionally ask about the name of our leadership training, coaching, and consulting firm, E Pluribus Partners. It is a nod to "E pluribus unum," the original motto of the United States, which means "out of many, one" in Latin. We chose this unusual-looking and tricky to pronounce phrase because it reflects how connection enables the best of what the *many* bring for the benefit of the collective *one*.

It's interesting to note how other languages capture a similar notion. The French phrase *esprit de corps*, for example, literally means "the spirit of the body." In certain countries in Africa *ubuntu* refers to one's connection to the community. At one of our seminars, a Japanese woman taught us that the Japanese call connection *ittaikan*, which means "to feel as one body of people." Connection is a universal phenomenon.

The previous chapter defined connection in the workplace as a bond among people based on shared identity, empathy, and understanding, moving primarily *self*-centered individuals toward *group*-centered membership. Let's unpack these concepts.

Identity is how people think of themselves—it's their story or narrative, including their values, reputation, and mission, if they have one. When people share an identity that inspires them and makes them feel proud, it creates a sense of connection, community, and unity among the members of the group.

Shared empathy is increased when people get to know and care for one another. Valuing people in and of themselves, rather than as means to an end, is key. Emotions are contagious, so as empathy increases people become more sensitive to the feelings of others, and as a result become more considerate and compassionate (Hatfield et al. 1994).

Shared understanding arises when members of a group are in the know, so to speak. They are informed on matters important to them, and their opinions and ideas are sought and considered. In other words, when there is an abundance of conversation and communication within a group, it produces a high degree of knowledge flow that results in shared understanding.

To make it easy to remember shared identity, shared empathy, and shared understanding, our colleague Carolyn Dewing-Hommes came up with nomenclature that represents the same ideas. Hereafter we will refer to shared identity, empathy, and understanding as vision, value, and voice, respectively.

## ASSESSING THE HEALTH OF YOUR WORK CULTURE

When we first began researching employee engagement and organizational effectiveness, we interviewed individuals and asked them to consider their own work (or volunteer) experiences in answering the following:

Think of a time when you felt fired up at work. Now write down the list of elements in the work culture that made you feel that way. After you've completed your list, consider a time when you felt like you were burning out. Write down the elements in the culture that made you feel that way.

A common response was, "I clicked with or felt connected to my work, my supervisor, my colleagues, and/or my organization (its mission, values, reputation)." More often than not, these individuals were describing an emotional reaction (how they felt). After consistently hearing that people felt connected at work in these various ways, we identified the factors that were making people feel a sense of connection at work.

The following are typical responses, along with commentary explaining the rationale for categorizing them under vision, value, or voice. Phrases preceded by a (+) sign are elements associated with a positive culture and those preceded by a (–) sign are elements associated with a negative culture. As you read through the lists, you might want to put a checkmark next to statements that resonate with you in the context of your current job.

## VISION
Inspiring identity that produces shared identity.

+ "Creating something new or doing something bigger than ourselves."

+ "We created something of lasting value."

+ "We had a clear strategy and direction with a common mission and goals."

+ "Having a shared vision about how we could succeed."

+ "I could make a difference in my role."

+ "We had values I cared about and that we lived up to (not just window dressing)."

+ "I felt proud to tell my family and friends that I worked at this organization."

- "Our work had no purpose."

- "Hard to see value of work."

- "There were too many priorities that were constantly changing."

- "There were unrealistic goals and expectations."

- "There was a lack of focus and goals were not aligned."

- "Feeling uncertain about the organization's future."

The positive responses reflect a sense of shared experience and identity. People felt connected to their work because of the group's focused effort, and their individual contribution made a meaningful difference. In the most powerful connecting experiences, the work of the group improved the lives of others by bringing goodness (such as a nurse's work that reflected goodness through healing), beauty (such as the technology product designer who created something well designed and functional), and truth (such as a teacher who brought knowledge and insight to students). A sense of shared identity develops among group members as their attitudes, language, and behaviors communicate the importance of the work, how the work is done in a way that reflects shared values, and how the work is producing positive results.

## VALUE

Human value that produces shared empathy.

+ "There was mutual respect and leaders cared about people first."

+ "Leaders did the right thing . . . they were ethical."

+ "We had autonomy and were trusted and empowered to make decisions."

+ "My role fit my interest and strengths."
+ "My supervisor cared about me as a person and helped me learn, develop, and grow."
+ "Supportive boss."
+ "We had fun."

- "The work was repetitive."
- "There was a lack of recognition."
- "I was micromanaged."
- "We were overworked and had little work-life balance."
- "There was no clear career progress."
- "No team support."
- "Work was not challenging enough."

The positive responses show that people feel valued as human beings, rather than being treated as means to an end. They had supervisors and leaders who cared about them, took time to get to know them, and helped them get into the right roles so they could continue to learn and grow. These leaders encouraged people when they did good work, gave them autonomy, and kept them challenged, but didn't chronically overload them with so much work that they had no work-life balance. The people they worked with valued them too. A sense of shared empathy develops among group members as their attitudes, language, and behaviors communicate to each person that she is valued as a person, and not merely for her work.

## VOICE

Knowledge flow that produces shared understanding.

+ "It was safe to speak, to disagree, to try new things and be myself."
+ "My opinion counted."

+ "It was a creative and innovative work environment."

+ "There were no hidden agendas."

+ "We were kept in the loop."

+ "People were open and spoke the truth."

+ "Relationally safe."

− "We were kept in the dark; there was a lack of communication."

− "I was expected to follow orders; my opinion wasn't considered and didn't matter."

− "People competed rather than collaborated with one another."

− "Feedback was infrequent."

− "Poor communication."

− "Not being listened to."

− "Lack of open-mindedness."

The positive responses reflect people who believed that they were kept informed about important matters and had a voice—their opinions and ideas were sought and considered. They also appreciated the openness of their culture and the open-mindedness of leaders. A sense of shared understanding develops among group members as their attitudes, language, and behaviors increase communication and bring greater clarity to issues that are important to individual members.

## TASK EXCELLENCE AND RESULTS

+ "Our work was done with excellence."

+ "We could see that we were making progress in our work."

+ "We delivered positive results."

+ "We hired talented people."

+ "We had high standards."

+ "Completing tasks, getting stuff done."

+ "Celebrating milestones."

- "There was no sense of accomplishment."

- "We were not stretching ourselves."

- "People I worked with didn't care."

- "I didn't have the resources and training I needed to do my work well."

- "My supervisor wouldn't deal with obstacles that prevented me from doing my work well."

- "Uncommitted management."

- "Excessive process, red tape, bureaucracy, and politics that impede progress."

The positive responses reflect a passion for excellence. When people worked with competent colleagues, their work was held to high standards and they produced positive results. This contributed to the sense of connection among employees.

## VISION + VALUE + VOICE = CONNECTION

The first element of a connection culture is vision. It exists in a culture when everyone is motivated by the mission, united by the values, and proud of the reputation. When people share a purpose or set of beliefs it unites and motivates them. At Memorial Sloan Kettering Cancer Center they are united and motivated by the aspiration stated in their tagline, "the best cancer care, anywhere," and the organization's reputation as one of the leading cancer centers in the world.

The following is one of my favorite examples of a brilliant leader's desire to instill vision in a company. During World War II, U.S. president Franklin D. Roosevelt traveled to Seattle, Washington, to meet with 18,000 aircraft workers at Boeing Corporation. He brought along Hewitt Wheless, a young airplane pilot from Texas who had escaped death thanks to the resilience of the bullet-riddled B-17 plane he flew out of harm's way. His plane had been built at that very Boeing plant. Seeing and hearing that young pilot thank them for saving his life connected the aircraft workers to a common cause. It transformed those welders and riveters into freedom fighters. From 1941 until 1945 American aircraft companies out-produced the Nazis three to one, building nearly 300,000 airplanes (Kearns Goodwin 1994).

Vision is more than identifying and articulating a mission. It also includes understanding how an organization goes about accomplishing its mission. In other words, vision encompasses the organization's values or beliefs about what is right and, by implication, what isn't right in how it conducts its business. The late Dame Anita Roddick communicated an inspiring vision when she founded and led The Body Shop to sell all-natural cosmetic products. What made The Body Shop different was that its products were environmentally friendly, didn't rely on animal testing, and were produced by women-owned businesses in developing countries. Roddick wanted to help women in developing countries by selling products to women in more affluent countries, and her vision was so compelling that it attracted scores of employees and customers. Under Roddick's leadership The Body Shop grew by 50 percent a year for years, even through a recession (Burlingham 1990; Carney 2005).

## VISION + **VALUE** + VOICE = CONNECTION

The second element of a connection culture is value. It means that people are truly valued as individuals, not merely for what they produce. Value exists in a culture when everyone in an organization understands universal human needs, appreciates the unique contribution of all members, and helps them achieve their potential.

In leading the turnaround of Dun and Bradstreet, Allan Loren established a rule that no meeting would be scheduled on Mondays or Fridays if it required people to travel over the weekend. He cared for people enough to protect their personal time. Loren also wanted to see people grow, so he implemented a program that matched everyone in the organization with a mentor who would provide continuous performance feedback. Mentors were selected based on their strengths in those areas that a particular employee wanted to improve upon.

Head of The Tata Group until he retired in 2012, Ratan Tata's response to the November 26, 2008, terrorist attack on the Tata-owned Taj Mahal Palace and Tower Hotel in Mumbai, India, showed how much he valued his employees. Dependents of the 80 employees who were affected were flown to Mumbai and housed for three weeks. Tata personally visited all of their families and attended the funerals of those who died. He also provided counseling for his employees and their families and forgave any outstanding loans to the affected employees. In addition, he established a trust fund so that dependents of those who died would continue to receive the deceased person's salary for life, the education of his or her children and dependents would be paid for, and the families would receive healthcare for the remainder of their lives.

Founded in 1877 and based in Mumbai, The Tata Group is one of the most respected organizations in the world. The "Tata family" comprises more than 450,000 people working in more than 100 diverse operating companies. It conducts business the "Tata Way," which prioritizes people and social responsibility over profit maximization. Tata was one of the first businesses to institute an eight-hour workday and distributes so much of its profit to philanthropic causes that some critics have questioned whether this generosity is wise. In answer to this criticism, Ratan Tata responded, "I would like to think this is the best part of what Tata stands for. . . . We really do care."

## VISION + VALUE + **VOICE** = CONNECTION

The third element of a connection culture is voice. It exists when everyone in an organization seeks the ideas and opinions of others, shares opinions honestly, and safeguards relational connections. In a culture in which voice exists, decision makers have the humility to know that they don't have a monopoly on good ideas, and they need to seek and consider the opinions and ideas of others in order to make the best decisions. When people's ideas and opinions are sought and considered, it helps meet the human needs for respect, recognition, and belonging. Being in the loop makes people feel connected to their colleagues, whereas being out of the loop does the opposite.

Terri Kelly is the CEO of W.L. Gore & Associates, a privately held company that creates a variety of innovative solutions—from medical devices to GORE-TEX fabrics. Powered by the element of voice, Kelly and her colleagues have created an engine of innovation in the company's connection culture. Instead of the traditional hierarchical management model, there are no formal titles or bosses, employees self-commit to what they want to work on, and leaders are selected by their peers. Kelly describes W.L. Gore as a "lattice or a network, and associates can go directly to anyone in the organization to get what they need to be successful." This may sound chaotic, but it has proven effective. W.L. Gore has been profitable every year since its founding in 1958. *Fortune* has consistently ranked the company as one of the "best places to work" and *Fast Company* labeled it as "the world's most innovative company" (Hamel 2012).

When Anne Mulcahy was appointed CEO of Xerox Corporation in 2000, the company was nearly broke and the company's lawyers and financial advisers told her to file for bankruptcy protection. She refused. Instead, she hit the road to meet with Xerox employees and customers, logging 100,000 miles of travel her first year. She was open and told them what she thought had to be done, even telling Wall Street analysts that the Xerox business model was unsustainable, which precipitated a 26 percent drop in the value of Xerox stock the following day. Mulcahy shared the good, the bad, and the ugly with her employees, solicited their ideas and opinions, and implemented the best ones. During the next decade, Mulcahy and her colleagues brought Xerox back to life. One Xerox board member described it as a miracle.

## THE CHARACTER CONNECTION

*Fired Up or Burned Out* introduced the concept and practices of a connection culture. Gathering and reviewing the research for that book inspired an aha moment when it revealed a clear link between certain character strengths and the elements of a connection culture. I was studying the field of positive psychology and the 24 character strengths. Positive psychologists believe that these ubiquitous, if not universal, character strengths, which have been favorably viewed by religious thinkers and moral philosophers throughout history, improve mental and physical health, and favor the survival of civilizations.

These 24 character strengths also favor the survival of organizations. For example, when individuals possess bravery, creativity, curiosity, honesty, humility, judgment, love of learning, perspective, and prudence, voice is present in a culture. The Character > Connection > Thrive Chain (Figure 2-1) shows how everything fits together, and descriptions of the 24 character strengths can be found in Appendix I.

FIGURE 2-1. THE CHARACTER > CONNECTION > THRIVE CHAIN

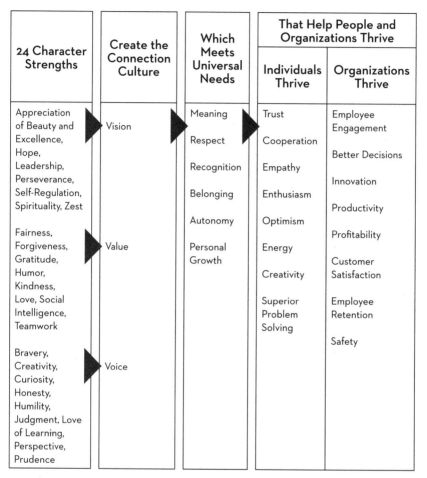

| 24 Character Strengths | Create the Connection Culture | Which Meets Universal Needs | That Help People and Organizations Thrive | |
|---|---|---|---|---|
| | | | Individuals Thrive | Organizations Thrive |
| Appreciation of Beauty and Excellence, Hope, Leadership, Perseverance, Self-Regulation, Spirituality, Zest | Vision | Meaning Respect Recognition Belonging Autonomy | Trust Cooperation Empathy Enthusiasm Optimism | Employee Engagement Better Decisions Innovation Productivity Profitability |
| Fairness, Forgiveness, Gratitude, Humor, Kindness, Love, Social Intelligence, Teamwork | Value | Personal Growth | Energy Creativity Superior Problem Solving | Customer Satisfaction Employee Retention Safety |
| Bravery, Creativity, Curiosity, Honesty, Humility, Judgment, Love of Learning, Perspective, Prudence | Voice | | | |

The 24 character strengths are found in belief systems that have been sustained for long periods of time, including Christianity, Judaism, Islam, Taoism, and Buddhism. Hate groups are the most common group to reject them. These groups often masquerade as a major religion in name, but certainly not in deed. For example, Adolf Hitler promoted "Positive Christianity." However, his message and actions were utterly at odds with Jesus's teaching to love, serve others, and be humble. Most religions have renegade branches that promote hate. These groups may thrive for a time, but eventually collapse for a lack of human value (the very heart of a connection culture).

Many individuals have observed the importance of character to human flourishing. David McCullough (1991), the Pulitzer Prize–winning author and historian, wrote: "While there are indeed great, often unfathomable forces in history before which even the most exceptional of individuals seem insignificant, the wonder is how often events turn upon a single personality, or the quality we call character." In one of his most memorable speeches, Rev. Martin Luther King Jr. shared that he dreamed of a day when his four young children would "live in a nation where they will not be judged by the color of their skin but by the content of their character."

John Wooden, the legendary coach of the UCLA men's basketball team, frequently taught his players that "ability may get you to the top, but only character will keep you there" (Wooden 1997). His observation that both ability and character are necessary to perform at the top of your game is similar to the connection culture model: task excellence + relationship excellence (connection) = sustainable superior performance. When coaching, Wooden used a system of character strengths called the "Pyramid of Success," which included industriousness, enthusiasm, friendship, loyalty, cooperation, self-control, alertness, initiative, intentness, condition, skill, and team spirit. He taught his players that believing and behaving in a way consistent with these character values produced poise and confidence that resulted in competitive greatness (that is, the desire to continuously challenge oneself in life). Patience and faith make up the mortar that holds the blocks together. Once the pyramid was built, it meant that the player met Wooden's standards and he earned the right to be called a member of the UCLA basketball team.

## THE PEOPLE WHO MAKE A CONNECTION CULTURE HAPPEN

Vision, value, and voice are the core elements of a connection culture. The people who bring these elements to a culture and make it happen are the enablers of the connection culture model and are called *committed members* and *servant leaders*. Committed members are committed to task excellence, promoting the connection culture, and living out character strengths and virtues. They may be senior managers, receptionists, salespeople, engineers, information technology experts, or customer service representatives. Servant leaders are committed members who have the authority to coordinate task excellence, facilitate the connection culture, and model and mentor others in character strengths and virtues.

Employees can only become servant leaders after becoming committed members. In other words, there needs to be proof of a commitment to achieving task excellence and a connection culture, and of the requisite character traits, before being given the authority to lead. With leadership authority comes the responsibility for modeling character strengths and virtues, as well as mentoring others. Servant leaders are serious about modeling and mentoring others because they were shaped by the individuals who modeled servant leadership and mentored them.

But why use the term *servant* to describe the type of leader who creates a connection culture? Because the very best leaders have the mindset that they are serving a cause greater than themselves, as well as serving the people they lead to achieve the cause. In other words, they are focused on achieving the mission, rather than glorifying themselves.

## A CULTURE OF CONNECTION

Committed members and servant leaders develop task excellence and relationship excellence that includes vision, value, and voice. As a result, people feel connected, are more productive and energetic, give their best efforts, align their efforts with organizational objectives, and fully communicate and cooperate. This leads the organization to achieve sustainable superior performance (Figure 2-2).

FIGURE 2-2. THE CONNECTION CULTURE

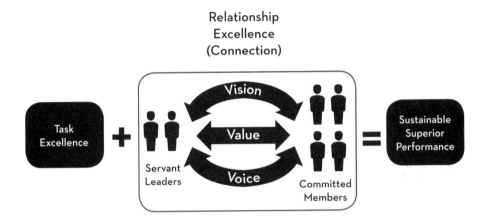

Organizations also have character. They reflect the collective character of their people, and especially that of their leaders. An organization's annual report may say its values include integrity and honesty, but if its employees don't follow those values, they are either frauds or, more likely, blind to their own character deficiencies. Great leaders are not only intentional about connecting, they are intentional about developing their own character and the character of the people they are responsible for leading.

Much has been written about the culture of Southwest Airlines. It is the largest domestic U.S. airline and still has an enviable record of profit in an industry that Warren Buffett once joked hadn't made a cumulative profit since the Wright brothers' first flight at Kitty Hawk in 1903. Southwest Airlines prides itself on its culture of putting people first and treating passengers like family. Its leaders learned from experience that connection affects performance. For example, Southwest maintains a 10-to-1 frontline-employee-to-supervisor ratio, which allows supervisors to connect with, coach, and encourage people. This has vastly improved their gate performance ratings. By contrast, some airlines have frontline-employee-to-supervisor ratios of 40-to-1, making connection very difficult to maintain (Maruca 2006).

Today Southwest's culture services department has 31 full-time employees, including eight culture ambassadors who are embedded within different operational departments. Furthermore, the company's 160 company-wide culture committee members are also spread throughout the organization. Southwest Airlines holds its culture in such high esteem that the "C" is always capitalized to signify that it is a word of importance. The airline also keeps its values visible to all employees. To encourage everyone to live up to them, two to three stories that celebrate employees who live out the values are posted each business day on the company intranet.

## DISCONNECTION: A CULTURE OF CONTROL OR A CULTURE OF INDIFFERENCE

What happens without a connection culture? While task excellence may be present for a while, in cultures of control or indifference most managers and employees put up self-protective barriers that keep them from performing at the top of their game. The disconnection sabotages task excellence and the organization suffers too (Figure 2-3).

## FIGURE 2-3. CULTURES OF CONTROL AND INDIFFERENCE

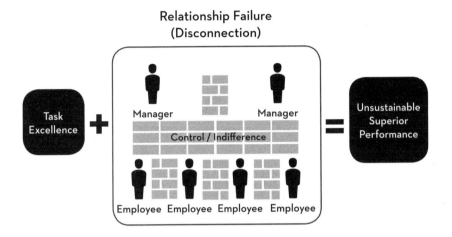

Leaders who foster cultures of control or cultures of indifference may succeed for a while, but their success is built on feet of clay that will inevitably crumble. History is filled with examples of this recurring theme. Could there be a better example than Enron, an energy, commodities, and services company whose leaders nurtured a dog-eat-dog environment and traders boasted about their power to make grandmothers in California suffer from electricity rate increases and power outages? Enron went bankrupt in 2001.

Our heroes are the leaders who create connection and bring vision, value, and voice to the people they lead. Wherever you find great nations, companies, nonprofits, and sports teams, you will find these great men and women.

# 3
# CONNECTION:
# HIDDEN IN PLAIN SIGHT

---

In this chapter you will learn:

- how leaders in various organizations and industries have fostered connection cultures

- the influence that connection cultures have had on organizations around the world.

---

Consider the wind. We cannot see it, but we can see its effect on trees when the wind blows through them. Similarly, we see the effect of connection on individuals, teams, and organizations. When connection is present people are more enthusiastic, cooperative, creative, and productive. When connection is absent they lack these traits.

Once you begin to truly understand connection, you'll see it everywhere. When you examine success stories through the lens of the connection culture framework, you'll be inspired by what leaders are doing in other sectors. The following stories feature inspiring leaders from business, government, healthcare, higher education, technology, faith-based communities, sports, and the social sectors.

## ALAN MULALLY'S ENCORE

When Alan Mulally was introduced as the next CEO of Ford Motor Company in 2006, he stunned the audience by candidly answering the question "what kind of car do you drive" with the response, "a Lexus . . . the finest car in the world." The room fell silent. Mulally's tenure as CEO of Ford was also full of surprises, particularly the remarkable turnaround he orchestrated.

The year Mulally arrived at Ford, sales, market share, and profits were falling, and the automaker's culture comprised silo rivalries with leaders embroiled in turf wars. This culture drove Ford to the verge of bankruptcy. By the time Mulally announced his retirement in May 2014, he had led Ford to 19 consecutive profitable quarters and rising market share in North America. And unlike American rivals General Motors and Chrysler, Ford did not seek a U.S. government bailout following the financial crisis in 2008. At his retirement, rather than the stunned silence Mulally experienced when first introduced, Ford employees gave him a standing ovation.

Alan Mulally is an excellent example of a leader who created a connection culture. He used founder Henry Ford's original vision of "opening the highways for all mankind" to express how the company makes the world a better place by serving others. Mulally explained that Ford gives people freedom of mobility so they can access opportunities for growth. This united employees around the vision and focused them on a cause greater than self. The vision was also factored into decision-making processes, such as in evaluations of new product development. The newly designed F-150 pickup, for example, got an aluminum-based body that made it lighter, more fuel efficient, and more affordable.

Mulally also boosted value in the Ford culture. He frequently used the phrases "One Ford," "one team," "the power of teams," and "working together always works." He also distributed wallet-sized cards with Ford's business plan on one side and 16 expected behaviors (values), including "work together effectively as one team," on the other. In meetings, he acted as a facilitator and coach rather than a dictator, prohibiting humor made at the expense of others. Rather than thinking of other individuals and organizations as competitors, Mulally employed a "win-win" approach to external relationships. This helped him forge an agreement with the United Auto Workers union to make the changes necessary for Ford to make a profit in return for bringing production back to the United States. It also helped him consolidate Ford's purchases to suppliers that were willing to partner with Ford to drive down costs in return for receiving a greater share of Ford's business.

Mulally expected leaders to openly share the obstacles they faced, and celebrated leaders who helped one another instead of focusing solely on problems in their domain. Another way he increased voice was through the weekly business plan review (BPR) meeting. Held at Ford's global headquarters in Dearborn, Michigan, the BPR is attended by the global leadership team and all business and functional leaders, either in person or by teleconference. At BPR meetings leaders give updates on their goals, which are color-coded green for on-target, yellow for at-risk, and red for off-target. When problems are identified, follow-up meetings are scheduled to dig deeper and identify solutions. BPRs also address strategic topics, such as the economy, labor supply, and competitive developments. Feedback is encouraged during BPRs, which have a safe environment for honest dialogue. This prompts people to move toward consensus, rather than forcing it, as well as helping decision makers identify optimal solutions, making alignment and excellence in execution more likely.

## RESTORING NAVY PRIDE

A leader in government and the military who intentionally developed a connection culture is Adm. Vernon Clark, the chief of naval operations (CNO) from 2000 until his retirement in 2005.

The CNO is the head of the U.S. Navy and the principal naval adviser to the U.S. president on the conduct of war. When Admiral Clark assumed the CNO role, the navy was not meeting its sailor retention goals, which is problematic when you consider the navy's sophisticated surveillance, navigation, and weapons systems, and the importance of maintaining the readiness of national defense. Concerned about how this would affect military preparedness, Clark made winning the war for talent his number one priority.

Admiral Clark increased vision by reminding sailors that the navy's mission is to take the war-fighting readiness of the United States to any corner of the world at a moment's notice. He said that it was time to build a modern navy that would be "strategically and operationally agile, technologically and organizationally innovative, networked at every level, highly joint [with the other services], and effectively integrated with allies" (Clark 2002).

Admiral Clark would tell sailors: What we do matters. What we do is hard work. We intentionally put ourselves in harm's way. We are away from our loved ones for months on end. We do it because it's important and we are people of service. We are committed to something larger than ourselves: the protection of America's interests around the world and democracy (U.S. Navy 2005). This made them feel proud and connected to him as their leader. Rear Adm. Frank Thorp, who served on Admiral Clark's personal staff, recounted an occasion when he spotted a sailor with tear-filled eyes after hearing Clark speak. Thorp approached the young man to see what was wrong. The sailor said he was going to ask his commanding officer to rip up the discharge papers he had recently submitted, because for the first time a leader had told him why he should stay in the navy (Herdt et al. 2008-2010).

Admiral Clark strongly supported an increase in pay that was approved by the president and Congress. When navy budget officials proposed cuts related to training and developing people as part of the annual planning cycle, Clark wouldn't allow it. Instead, he increased the training budget. As part of what he called the revolution in training, Admiral Clark established the Naval Education and Training Command and required everyone in the navy to have a personal development plan. He changed the performance appraisal system to provide constructive feedback for everyone, and added the requirement to leaders' performance appraisals that they help sailors learn and grow. He valued personal growth and continuous improvement, saying, "if you are not growing, in my view, you are of little value to the institution. . . . if you are not growing, you're dead" (Clark 2003).

In the navy, enlisted sailors sometimes feel like second-class citizens compared to the officers. Admiral Clark made it one of his priorities to blur some of the lines between the officers and enlisted sailors, while still maintaining the necessary decision-making chain of command. When he traveled to commands and bases around the world, Clark met with commanding officers, as well as the master chiefs, their enlisted counterparts. He intentionally reached out to the master chiefs because he valued them and what they could do for the sailors under their leadership. He told them, these young sailors under our command swear to support and defend the U.S. Constitution from all enemies and we as leaders need to make promises in return. We need to give them the training and resources to enable them to fulfill their promise. We need to give them an opportunity to prove what they can do (Herdt et al. 2008-2010).

Admiral Clark recognized the importance of the enlisted leaders because of his own experiences as a sailor. He often told a story of his first experience on a ship following officer candidate school.

> I didn't know the pointy end of the ship from the blunt
> end. It was scary, really. But fortunately there was a master

chief there who took a liking to me, Master Chief Leedy. For some reason, I don't know what possessed him, but after I had been there about a week he came up to me, and put his arm around me, and he said, "Mr. Clark, I'm going to help make you into a fine officer." (Herdt et al. 2008-2010)

The advice and encouragement from Master Chief Leedy helped make Clark a better officer. He said that he, and our country, needed the master chiefs to mentor and encourage today's young sailors in the same way. They listened—Master Chief Petty Officer of the Navy Jim Herdt once said that master chiefs around the world had the general attitude that "Old Vern is counting on us and we can't let him down" (Herdt et al. 2008-2010). He made them feel valued, and when they reached out to help those under their command learn and grow, the sailors felt valued too.

Clark also worked to change the legacy systems that devalued sailors, such as the navy's job assignment process. Under Clark and a program he dubbed "the revolution in personnel distribution," the system was changed to a job bidding approach, with incentive compensation for the jobs and locations that were least in demand. As a result, the percentage of sailors forced into positions or locations they didn't want was reduced from 30 percent to around 1.5 percent.

In group meetings with leaders, Admiral Clark encouraged participants to speak up. His own approachable, conversational style set the tone for others to share their ideas and opinions. He asked everyone to "challenge every assumption," "be data driven," and "drill down" into the details. He challenged them to "have a sense of urgency to make the navy better every day" in order to deliver greater efficiencies and readiness for the dollars America invested in the navy (Herdt et al. 2008-2010).

Clark was more concerned about getting it right than being right himself. He encouraged "constructive friction," which he said made it safe for people to disagree and express views that were outside the consensus. As a result, Clark's leaders felt connected with him and the U.S. Navy, and they emulated his leadership style, which made the sailors under their command feel more connected.

Admiral Clark is quick to say that he's not perfect. Nonetheless, the navy achieved some impressive gains during his tenure as CNO and many naval leaders have praised his leadership and positive influence. In a little more than a year after Clark became CNO, first term re-enlistment soared from less than 38 percent to 56.7 percent (Herdt et al. 2008-2010).

As the navy improved sailor retention and developed greater alignment with Admiral Clark's vision, it became faster and more responsive. Within a matter of hours following the terrorist attacks on September 11, 2001, aircraft carriers, Aegis destroyers, and cruisers were in position to protect America's shores. This was partially due to the fact that naval leaders anticipated what had to be done and took action before they received orders. After the Pentagon was attacked communications and the navy's decision-making process were quickly re-established, and planning for America's response began while the embers of the fire still smoldered a short distance away.

## SAVING THE GIRL SCOUTS

There was a time in the mid-1970s when the Girl Scouts were struggling and their future looked uncertain. Fortunately, Frances Hesselbein came to the rescue. Hesselbein began her association with the Girl Scouts when she agreed to lead a troop of 30 girls in Johnstown, Pennsylvania, whose leader had recently left. Although she had no daughters of her own, it wasn't long before her experience with Troop 17 developed into a lifelong commitment to Girl Scouting. In 1976, she became CEO of the national organization.

With membership falling and the organization in a state of serious decline, Hesselbein put sound management practices in place. During her 24-year tenure, Girl Scout membership quadrupled to nearly 3.5 million, diversity more than tripled, and the organization was transformed into what Peter Drucker described as "the best-managed organization around." She accomplished this amazing turnaround with 6,000 paid staff members and 730,000 volunteers. Her use of connection culture put the Girl Scouts on track for success.

Hesselbein stressed the importance of reaching out to scouts and educating them about the threats they face, such as drugs and teen pregnancy. She helped women to envision the Girl Scouts as a professional, well-managed organization that could carry out this important work.

Hesselbein's leadership style boosted the culture's value. She once wrote that effective leaders have a genuine "appreciation of their colleagues individually and the dignity of the work their colleagues do" (Hesselbein 2002, 32). Hesselbein's leadership philosophy is "to serve is to live" and her words and actions embody human value. She built a conference center to train Girl Scout staff and invested in improving Girl Scout leaders' people skills. As a role model, she effectively increased human value in the Girl Scout culture and multiplied her actions as other leaders across the organization adopted her leadership style. She kept up with what was going on in the lives of the people around her and personally reached out to anyone when congratulations or consolation were in order.

Voice is key to innovation because it creates a marketplace of ideas that allows people to more easily spot new opportunities to improve the organization. Hesselbein increased this value by approaching communication in an inclusive way, expanding information in ever-larger circles across the organization. Rather than lecturing, her style was to ask insightful questions to draw out relevant issues. In planning and allocating the Girl Scouts's resources, she introduced a circular management process that involved nearly everyone within the organization.

By the time Hesselbein resigned in 1990, the Girl Scouts's future was bright. She was able to continue spreading her leadership legacy when Peter Drucker recruited her to be the head of the Drucker Foundation (which was renamed the Leader to Leader Institute, and more recently the Frances Hesselbein Leadership Institute). Through its activities, including publication of the award-winning *Leader to Leader* journal, the institute is dedicated to carrying out the passion that Drucker and Hesselbein shared for strengthening leadership in the social sector. That dedication was further recognized in 1998 when she was awarded the Presidential Medal of Freedom by President Bill Clinton for her work as "a pioneer for women, volunteerism, diversity, and opportunity."

## COACH K'S AHA MOMENT

Mike Krzyzewski, Coach K, as he is better known, has regularly led the Duke University men's basketball team to the Final Four of American college basketball. Consider what he's accomplished:

- four national championships (1991, 1992, 2001, 2010)
- four Olympic gold medals as head coach of the U.S. men's national team
- 983 career wins (the most in NCAA history).

One look at his 14-page biography on the Duke website is all one needs to truly appreciate the magnitude of his accomplishments. Coach K's phenomenal success as a coach and leader begs the question: How does he do it?

The obvious reasons are that he's talented, disciplined, and works hard. But a lot of coaches fit that description, so there must be something else that separates Coach K from other coaches and provides his team with a sustainable competitive advantage.

Coach K grew up in a male-dominated culture. He attended an all-boys Catholic high school in Chicago, and then went on to play basketball at West Point under the driven, domineering, and perfectionist coach Bobby Knight. He also served in the U.S. Army.

Then his outlook took a major turn when he found himself outnumbered at home by his wife, Mickie, and their three daughters. Every night at dinner Coach K observed how Mickie and the girls reconnected by sharing the details of their day, including what they had done and how they felt about it. Whereas guys often cut to the chase in conversations, his wife and daughters invested time each day to reconnect.

He also observed how attuned they were to how people felt—their intuition was like radar. Time and again Mickie could sense when something was bothering one of Coach K's players. She was nearly always right, so he learned that it was wise to follow up and ask the player if something was wrong. Sure enough, something was always amiss and talking about the problem made the player feel, and play, better. When he didn't follow up, the player often fell out of sync with the team and performance suffered.

Coach K's aha moment about the importance of connection and relationships transformed his coaching style. He began involving Mickie and his daughters in the Duke men's basketball program. The Krzyzewski women became, in military terms, a reconnaissance team to sense the state of relationships, emotions, connection, community, and unity among the team. The boys became extended members of their family—the women gave the players hugs (which boost the trust hormone oxytocin). As Coach K became more intentional about developing the feeling of connection among the team, it produced superior results. He stressed the importance of knowing everyone's name and being courteous to fellow players: "You know what? 'Please' and 'Thank you' go a long way. You can be damn sure that every guy on my team says that. The best way to get better as a team is if everyone has ownership, and if you do these things they will" (Sokolove 2006).

If you study Coach K's approach you'll see that he clearly articulates a connection culture in which shared identity, empathy, and understanding move primarily self-centered individuals toward group-centered membership. When speaking to potential recruits Coach K tells them, "We're developing a relationship here, and if you are not interested, tell me sooner rather than later. . . . If you come here, for however long, you're going to unpack your suitcase. We're going to form a bond, and you're going to be part of this family" (Sokolove 2006).

On the surface, this sounds easy. But it's not. Human beings are complex. They are driven consciously and unconsciously by an infinite variety of past experiences, temperaments, perspectives, and thinking and learning styles. Coach K and his coaching staff, including the Krzyzewski women, have been developing ways to connect for years. Whereas most coaches and leaders remain clueless to the power of connection, the Krzyzewskis continue refining their methods while adding to Coach K's legacy and the remarkable record of success of Duke's men's basketball program.

## HEALING CONNECTIONS

The best culture in a healthcare organization is a connection culture. Patients and their families benefit from the feeling of connection among healthcare professionals that extends to them and helps reduce the stress and anxiety that accompany illness.

Chapter 1 shared my family's experiences during my wife's battles with breast cancer and ovarian cancer. The healthcare workers we met were kind and compassionate and our whole family felt connected to everyone, from doctors and nurses to the environmental services staff and even the cafeteria workers. These connections helped us cope with the stress and anxiety from our concern about Katie's uncertain future and are an important part of the healthcare culture.

As mentioned, vision includes an organization's core beliefs about the ways it goes about doing its work (and, by inference, the ways it deems as unacceptable). For example, many healthcare organizations embrace the values of excellence, integrity, respect, and caring and compassion for patients and their families. The MD Anderson Cancer Center has a strong vision that is summarized in the phrase from its logo: "Making cancer history." MD Anderson has a reputation for being one of the best cancer centers in the world, and its vision is an enormous sense of pride to its employees.

When he was president and CEO of the not-for-profit New York–Presbyterian Hospital, Dr. Herbert Pardes was a great example of a leader who promoted value. A well-respected psychiatrist and former director of the National Institute of Mental Health, Pardes always devoted time to making bedside visits to patients, something that other leaders might dismiss as inefficient. But he was passionate about providing humane healthcare and understood that connection made patients and their families feel better.

Pardes valued his employees and put practices in place to ensure that the people who worked in his hospital were caring and engaged individuals. He advocated for personal and professional mentors, and strived to help his employees balance their personal lives with professional growth. To extend the feeling of connection, he encouraged staff members to memorize the names of patients and their family members.

By combining a connection culture with sound management practices, Pardes and his team turned around the hospital system—New York–Presbyterian's revenue rose from $1.7 billion in 1999 to $3.7 billion in 2011. Whereas most hospitals find it difficult to attract and retain nurses, New York–Presbyterian's vacancy rate was less than a third of the national average. The *New York Times* observed that while "most urban hospitals have struggled, New York–Presbyterian has thrived" (Stodghill 2007).

*Fired Up or Burned Out* talked about the late Dr. Fred Epstein, a world-famous pediatric neurosurgeon and founder of the Institute for Neurology and Neurosurgery (INN) at Beth Israel Hospital in New York City. He increased voice in INN's culture by reducing the degree of formality, and making doctors and staff more approachable: White coats were banned, everyone addressed doctors by their first names, and physicians, nurses, and other healthcare professionals were encouraged to collaborate rather than treating doctors as if they were better than everyone else.

## BEING GOOGLEY

Many leaders wonder if they need to make their employees happy, but it depends on how you define it. Happiness can be thought of in two ways: pleasure or human thriving. Let's look at both in the context of the work environment of Google.

Having spoken there, I can attest that few organizations match the pleasure that the Googleplex in Mountain View, California, brings to Google's employees. The beautiful campus setting includes office space with modern design elements and ample natural light, a health center, a health club, and on-site parks. And then there are the free gourmet food and snacks. Who wouldn't derive pleasure working in a place like that?

The abundance of creature comforts at Google, however, is not the primary engine that fires up the employees of this remarkable organization. The second type of happiness is key: Google fosters a culture where people thrive; one that's a classic example of a connection culture.

Google's vision is captured by its mission statement: "to organize the world's information and make it universally accessible and useful." *Googlers* (a term Google employees use for each other) understand that Google's products help change the world by making people smarter and better decision makers. This prospect keeps them motivated and engaged.

Google's motto, "Don't be evil," is a simple statement that recognizes the value of respect, fairness, honesty, transparency, and responsibility. Googlers connect with the firm's "Googley" style, which champions being authentic, genuine, fun, and curious. Being Googley ties in to the company's modern, bright, and colorful visual identity, which is incorporated into everything from its website and written materials to the office design and building architecture. Google is also one of the world's most innovative companies. It has a reputation for hiring smart people, and is globally recognized as one of the best companies to work for. This makes Googlers proud to be members of the organization.

A research project entitled "Project Oxygen" studied the technical supervisors that Google's engineers and scientists wanted to work for to identify why they were so valued. The research concluded that the supervisors made time for one-on-one meetings, helped them work through problems by asking questions rather than dictating answers, and were interested in their lives and careers.

Googlers feel valued when they learn and grow through training provided by Google, as well as the coaching and mentoring provided by their supervisors. In addition, they can take advantage of G2G (Googler to Googler) training, where in-house experts train their peers on everything from job-related topics to unrelated topics, such as a Bollywood dance class. Other benefits include flextime and telecommuting, employee network groups, maternity leave, and charitable gift matching.

TGIF meetings are all-hands meetings conducted by the Google founders and other members of the executive team every Friday, which give employees a sense of voice that makes them feel connected. Googlers vote on the questions they would like to see answered by the management team.

## ALPHA CHURCH

In the Kensington section of London, just down the street from Harrods department store and a stone's throw from the Victoria and Albert Museum, is a small, unassuming campus with a church from the 1800s, a few plain-looking buildings, and a charming park. One could pass by this tiny enclave and have no idea that it is the epicenter of an extraordinary global movement and the home of one of the most influential and effective churches in the world.

It is Holy Trinity Brompton (HTB), an Anglican parish that is the birthplace of the Alpha course, a 15-session, 10-week course that introduces participants to the core beliefs of the Christian faith in a relaxed and engaging way that welcomes wrestling with big questions, such as "What is the meaning of life?" and "Does God heal today?" The course includes a weekend away and a celebration at the end.

To say that the Alpha course has been successful would be an understatement—its global reach is breathtaking. Since its launch in the late 1980s, more than 24 million individuals have completed the course, which is supported by all major Christian denominations and is currently taught in 169 countries and 112 languages.

HTB has also expanded into three other satellite churches in the greater London area, and has initiated more than 20 church plants in historically significant churches that would otherwise close.

In 2011 Katie and I spent eight days at HTB with collaborators from Trinity Church in Greenwich, Connecticut, and its research and teaching arm, Trinity Institute. We attended the HTB Leadership Conference, several HTB worship services and programs, and internal staff meetings. We also met with more than a dozen HTB and Alpha International leaders in one-hour sessions. (HTB and its sister organization, Alpha International, are two distinct legal entities that for the most part operate as one socio-political culture, hereafter referred to as HTB.)

HTB's mission is "to play our part in the re-evangelisation of the world and the transformation of society" (Elsdon-Dew 2014). Striving to achieve this mission provides a powerful sense of purpose for those who work at HTB and its parishioners.

As people focus on day-to-day tasks it's easy to lose sight of the vision, so leaders need to regularly remind people that the vision is important and they are helping to achieve it. Several HTB leaders explained that "vision leaks," and thus must continuously be refilled. To that end, HTB holds a weekly all-staff meeting with approximately 250 individuals in attendance. It is somewhat like a worship service for HTB staff, because it includes time for fellowship over breakfast followed by worship and prayer. During the meeting we attended, at least 30 minutes of open mic time was allotted for individuals to share heartwarming and encouraging stories about how HTB was making a difference throughout the world. This is typical of many of the regularly scheduled weekly meetings at HTB, at which people connect with one another before getting into the work content of the meeting.

HTB's core values, including excellence, serving others, friendliness, and fun, serve to bring about feelings of connection. Individuals at HTB "aim for perfection but settle for excellence." Nicky Gumbel, HTB vicar, often says, "everyone prays, everyone serves, everyone gives." An HTB leader who focused on securing volunteers described HTB as a sailboat where everyone on board had an active role to play, versus a cruise ship where passengers were served but never served others. HTB's leaders and members generally are outgoing, have a sense of humor, and don't seem to take themselves too seriously.

Because HTB walks the talk in terms of its mission and core values, it has experienced outstanding growth and the successful spread of the Alpha course worldwide. As a result, HTB has developed an external reputation as one of the leading churches worldwide. This reputation reinforces their belief that they are participating in an important endeavor that is transforming the world.

HTB emphasizes living out the Bible's teachings on character strengths that improve relationships with others. These character strengths are both taught and caught as a result of mentoring and social immersion in the Christian community. Being part of a culture in which character strengths are lived out makes one personally feel valued and connected to the community.

No description of the HTB culture would be complete without recognizing that they are extremely social. This is important because the broader British culture has experienced a decline of social capital, increased loneliness, anxiety, and depression; HTB is an island of social activity, community, and joy that helps meet its members' needs for connection (Griffin 2010).

Leaders who work alongside Nicky Gumbel comment that he nearly always seeks the opinions of others before making decisions. The leaders are open and generous in sharing their ideas and opinions, and genuinely want to help Christians and churches that share their mission and values. HTB is regularly exposed to new ideas and practices being developed around the world and embraces the opportunity this presents. This attitude increases the flow of knowledge among individuals at HTB and other churches.

HTB continuously seeks feedback so that it might learn and grow. In addition to an annual congregational survey, debriefing sessions following HTB events are another consistent practice. These sessions provide a forum to reflect on what went right, what went wrong, and what was missing. Within minutes of the conclusion of the HTB Leadership Conference, we received an email survey seeking our opinions and ideas about the conference and how to improve it.

Ultimately the high degree of knowledge flow helps HTB make continuous progress toward the perfection it strives to achieve. The Alpha course is one such example. It took more than 15 years to develop, with continuous improvements made as fresh insights and ideas emerged from the many individuals involved with the Alpha courses. Even now HTB continues to make improvements and updates to keep the Alpha course fresh, relevant, and effective. In fact, giving people voice is one of the Alpha course's core values, in addition to praying for and loving the guests (as Alpha course attendees are called), which reflects the element of value.

## HORNED FROG FAMILY

Texas Christian University (TCU) is a university of 10,000 students located in Fort Worth, Texas. In recent years, TCU has been recognized as a top 100 *U.S. News & World Report* college and in the top 20 list of up-and-coming national universities. In 2015, TCU ranked 76—moving 37 places in the last six years. Its sports teams have been in the national spotlight too. TCU's football team appeared in the Fiesta Bowl in 2010, the Rose Bowl in 2011, and the Peach Bowl in 2014, and its baseball team went to the College World Series in 2010 and 2014.

As word about TCU has spread, applications have soared. Since 2011 the school has consistently received as many as 19,000 applications to fill 1,800 freshman openings each year, making it the second-most selective college in Texas behind Rice University. However, the attitude of TCU admissions officers is surprising. Although they're delighted that awareness of TCU is increasing, there is a genuine sense of empathy for the disappointment felt by many students they have to turn away.

Seeing TCU up close allows you to appreciate that its true strength—indeed its competitive advantage—is more than just academics and sports. What really makes TCU stand out is its connection culture.

TCU's formal vision is "to be a world-class, values-centered university" and its mission is "to educate individuals to think and act as ethical leaders and responsible citizens in the global community." The university values "academic achievement, personal freedom and integrity, the dignity of and respect for the individual, and a *deep heritage that includes inclusiveness and service*" [emphasis added]. Informally, this can be summarized by the phrase that appears beneath TCU's logo: Learning to change the world.

Valuing people is a signature character strength of TCU's culture. TCU faculty clearly value their students, and thanks to a student-teacher ratio of 13-to-1, faculty members have time to get to know them. The enthusiasm of its faculty members has helped raise TCU's status in the academic community. During the past four years, TCU was selected by the *Chronicle of Higher Education* as one of the top 100 Great Colleges to Work For, and it has been named to the Honor Roll each year for scoring well in more than four categories.

TCU chancellor Victor Boschini leads the culture in word and deed. In his 2011 University Convocation and Founders' Celebration address, Boschini said:

> One theme runs through all our achievements. From our record number of applications to our rankings, as well as our recognition as a "Hot School," as an up-and-coming university, and as a great place to work. That theme is TCU's culture of unity, connection, and community. (Boschini 2011)

An advocate of servant leadership, Boschini praises TCU's faculty and staff for continuing to "build the mentoring relationships that have long defined TCU." The university is intentional about hiring teacher-scholars who like mentoring students and who will involve them in their research activities—in fact, approximately 25 percent of the student body is doing research projects.

Boschini's mantra for 2011 was "listening," and he continues to carry this mantra today; he always appears to be curious about what people think. Outgoing, enthusiastic, and energetic, when he engages in conversation he is present and focused on the other person. To stay in touch with students, he teaches a freshman seminar in education. And he not only knows every student's name, but also what is going on in their lives.

Boschini places a high priority on the importance of students making friends and establishing a support network. TCU has myriad programs to help students make connections, even before the first day of class. Send-Off parties occur around the United States to connect incoming students and their parents with others from their region before they leave home. Frog Camps—whether held in Fort Worth, the mountains of Colorado, or in an international city—introduce new students to each other and to TCU's history and traditions. Frogs First helps new students connect through activities that establish a friendly tone around campus. There is also a Connections program that places students in small groups that meet during the fall semester and are led by upper classmen. Throughout the year, TCU's student affairs department orchestrates initiatives and events such as Community Renewal, Drum Café, water balloon slingshot shooting, Christmas tree lighting and fireworks, and even bounce houses out on the campus commons.

In an effort to ensure that its students spend four years immersed in cultures of connection, in 2014 TCU established the TCU Center for Connection Culture. Its mission is to further equip the TCU community to sustain a connection culture and to introduce those principles to the broader community.

Fort Worth embraces TCU as its university and the students embrace the city in return. Merchants display posters of TCU's sports teams, many residents fly TCU flags, and local street signs are TCU purple with small white icons of the horned frog mascot. The university's LEAPS program connects student volunteers with opportunities to serve.

As a final example of TCU's commitment to fostering connection, consider Frogs for the Cure, an organization dedicated to supporting those with breast cancer and helping to eradicate the disease. In 2005 TCU athletics partnered with Susan G. Komen Greater Fort Worth to sponsor the first-ever pink out halftime presentation at a university football game, starting the national trend to give tribute to survivors that is now commonplace on collegiate and professional athletic fields during Breast Cancer Awareness month. Under the dedicated and tireless leadership of Ann Louden, Chancellor's Associate for Strategic Partnerships and a cancer survivor, Frogs for the Cure has grown to a committee of 210 that includes students, staff and faculty, community leaders, and members of the medical community, who organize year-round activities.

The highlight of each year's Frogs for the Cure pink out halftime show is the special music video that plays on the stadium's jumbo screens. First created in 2010, the video combined inspirational music and footage of hundreds of survivors and supporters. With each subsequent year, the music video has become more elaborate. A natural connector, Louden uses the video to bring together local cancer survivors with students from all sorts of groups and teams on campus, TCU faculty and staff members, alumni, and local government leaders, including Fort Worth mayor Betsy Price. Even Mark Cuban, owner of the Dallas Mavericks, took part one year.

To mark the 10-year anniversary of Frogs for the Cure, the 2014 music video featured Josh Groban's recording of "Brave" and included scenes shot on TCU's campus, as well as in New York City, Washington, D.C., Chicago, and at the Rose Bowl in Los Angeles. Laura Bush endorsed the video, which debuted at a concert featuring CBS newsman Bob Schieffer's band, Honky Tonk Confidential, and headliner Bernadette Peters. Survivors who take part in the filming or go out onto the football field for the halftime show report that it is a life-affirming experience that helps them heal. My wife, Katie, can attest to this.

As TCU continues to educate and equip students to become intentional about connecting with others and influencing the cultures they are in, these students may indeed help change the world.

# 4

# THE SCIENTIFIC CASE
# FOR CONNECTION

---

In this chapter you will learn:

- the scientific case for connection as supported by the fields of psychology, sociology, neuroscience, and organizational management

- research on connection's impact on the health and performance of both individuals and organizations

- research on the current state of connection for both individuals and organizations.

---

Connection is a superpower. At least, that's how UCLA neuroscience professor Matthew Lieberman described connection in *Social: Why Our Brains Are Wired to Connect* and in his TED talk in October 2013.

Most people don't yet recognize connection as a superpower and therefore miss out on its benefits. In their defense, they may be living and working in cultures that have conditioned them not to see, feel, or experience connection as much as they should in order to live the most productive and enjoyable lives possible.

It should be noted that describing all the research on connection that's been collected or conducted over the years would require multiple volumes. This chapter features carefully curated research and evidence that's especially relevant to illustrate the power connection has to improve individual and organizational health and performance. To truly understand why organizations with high connection and employee engagement outperform other organizations, one must begin by discovering what makes individuals thrive.

## INDIVIDUAL WELLNESS, WELL-BEING, AND PERFORMANCE

When John Bowlby studied homeless and orphaned children following World War II, he found that children who experienced little or no connection developed emotional and behavioral problems (Karen 1990). Describing connection as "attachment," Bowlby's theories began a field of study called attachment theory, which he articulated in a three-volume work titled *Attachment and Loss* published in 1969, 1972, and 1980.

Mary Ainsworth, Bowlby's onetime student and eventual colleague, went on to conduct research on infants that identified patterns of connection that are formed in early childhood. The attachment patterns she identified were shown to affect the development of social skills, confidence, curiosity and exploratory behavior, enthusiasm, persistence in problem solving, and the ability to cope with ambiguity, change, and stress. Children with secure attachments developed well, whereas children with insecure attachments developed poorly (Karen 1990).

The environment in which a child is raised is not the sole determinant of human strengths or vulnerabilities; genetics also plays a role. Genes and the environment interact to affect emotions and behavior. In fact, scientists have come to believe that the environment in which people live alters gene expression. Because genes are inherited and environments affect gene expression, this means that your genes are shaped by the environments in which your mother and your father lived (Hurley 2013). Thus, the degree of connection your ancestors experienced is expressed in the genes that were passed on to you. With this in mind, putting yourself in healthy environments filled with positive connection not only benefits you in your lifetime, but will also benefit your descendants.

What neuroscience and endocrinology have discovered about connection is illuminating. Neuroscience studies the brain and nervous system, while endocrinology studies the hormones and glands that secrete them. Research shows that feelings of connection affect neurotransmitters (chemical messengers in the brain, including serotonin, dopamine, and norepinephrine), hormones (chemical messengers that travel throughout the body including adrenaline, cortisol, oxytocin, and vasopressin), and enzymes that affect chromosomes (such as telomerase). These biochemicals help us thrive and live longer. However, a lack of connection negatively affects them, and a sustained connection deficit can cause dysfunction and even increase the likelihood of premature death (Hallowell 1999; Sapolsky 2008, 2010).

We've seen the importance of connection affirmed in research on wellness and well-being. In their book *Wellbeing: The Five Essential Elements*, Tom Rath and James Harter discuss a holistic view of what contributes to well-being during a lifetime. The following are just a few of the positive influences that connection has:

- Individuals who have the highest well-being get an average of six hours of social time (connection) each day through face-to-face, telephone, email, and Internet interactions.

- The single best predictor of employee engagement is *who* people are with (connection), rather than *what* they are doing (tasks).

- Self-control and goal accomplishment are positively correlated to connection, especially in regard to diet and exercise. A study showed that a 10-month intensive weight-loss program was maintained only 24 percent of the time when undertaken alone, but had a success rate of 50 percent when undertaken with a group of three strangers and 66 percent when undertaken with three friends or colleagues.

The opposite of connection is feeling unsupported, left out, or lonely. In numerous peer-reviewed journals and his book *Loneliness: Human Nature and the Need for Social Connection*, University of Chicago's Center for Cognitive and Social Neuroscience director John T. Cacioppo has reinforced these views by helping better explain the effects of disconnection. He makes the important point that feeling connected is subjective—an individual may be surrounded by people throughout the day, yet still feel disconnected. According to Cacioppo, connection has three avenues: intimate connectedness with a soulmate, relational connectedness with family and friends, and collective connectedness with intermediate associations (which are groups we are not related to by blood, such as community, religious, or alumni organizations) (Cacioppo and Patrick 2008). When one of these three avenues of connection declines, feelings of stability and security diminish, and are often replaced by a sense of loneliness, which is frequently coupled with depression, although they are distinct experiences.

The most extreme feelings of disconnection come when people feel left out (referred to as social exclusion). Think of a time when you felt socially excluded. Perhaps it was during middle school or in your first semester of college. This feeling is particularly destructive. Research on the effects of social exclusion has found that it makes people more aggressive toward those who excluded them and toward innocent bystanders; results in self-defeating behavior, including excessive risk taking, procrastination, and unhealthy diets; reduces intelligent thought, including logic and reasoning skills; and diminishes willpower to persevere on frustrating tasks (Twenge et al. 2001; Baumeister et al. 2002, 2005; Olds and Schwartz 2009). In addition, the 10-year MacArthur Foundation Study of Successful Aging, which included dozens of research projects, found that social exclusion is a "powerful risk factor for poor health," social support has "direct positive effects on health," and social support can reduce the health-related effects of aging (Rowe and Kahn 1998).

When connection, wellness, and well-being are high, life span and achievement increase. The Harvard Grant Study, one of the longest-running studies of human flourishing, followed 268 male Harvard graduates beginning in 1938. It found that the warmth of relationships (connection) positively correlated with individual health, happiness, professional success, compensation, and longevity (Valliant 2012). In addition, a 20-year longitudinal study of 820 individuals showed that employees who experienced greater connection in the workplace had a 240 percent lower death rate. Researchers concluded that "only one main effect was found: the risk of mortality was significantly lower for those reporting peer social support" (Shirom et al. 2011).

Perhaps one of the most famous studies of the effect of connection within a community was the case of Roseto, Pennsylvania, which gave birth to the term the *Roseto Effect*. The predominantly Italian-American community, which Malcolm Gladwell wrote about in *Outliers*, had half the risk of death from heart attacks versus the overall U.S. population. In addition, the community had no suicides, alcoholism, or drug addiction, and very little crime. After ruling out other factors, including diet and environment, researchers concluded that the Rosetans' health and longevity benefitted from the high degree of connection within the community. They visited one another, participated in community groups, and in many households several generations lived together (Gladwell 2008; Bruhn and Wolf 1979).

Clearly, connection positively affects human wellness and well-being, including mental and physical health, performance, and longevity. Likewise, the evidence supports the conclusion that disconnection leads to dysfunction and, when sustained, even premature death.

## ORGANIZATIONAL HEALTH
## AND SUSTAINABILITY

In 2007 the Conference Board, a global independent business membership and research organization, asked its employee engagement and commitment working group, which was composed of 24 human resources and employee communications leaders, to come up with a definition for employee engagement. The group offered the following definition, which is consistent with our findings on connection and connection culture:

> Employee engagement is a heightened emotional and intellectual connection that an employee has for his/her job, organization, manager, or coworkers that, in turn, influences him/her to apply additional discretionary effort to his/her work. (Gibbons 2007)

Unfortunately, since 2000 nearly 75 percent of people working in the United States have been disengaged with their jobs (Gallup 2013b). Gallup developed the Q12 survey to measure engagement. Like other employee engagement surveys, the Q12 asks questions to assess your level of connection with your organization's mission and purpose, as well as with your supervisor and colleagues, such as whether your supervisor or colleagues care about you as a person, make their expectations clear, encourage your development, and consider your opinion. It also assesses whether you feel connected to your work, by asking whether your job is a good fit with your strengths and if you are learning and growing. The Q12 even asks if you have a best friend at work—a question that certainly affects connection, but is also one that many leaders struggle with because they believe it isn't reasonable to hold a leader accountable for delivering best friends at work.

In 2012 Gallup researched 49,929 business or work units, comprising 1.4 million employees within 192 organizations across

34 nations. Their findings were highlighted in chapter 1, and bear repeating. The research concluded that business units with higher Q12 scores (in other words, higher connection) experienced 21 percent higher productivity levels, 22 percent higher profitability, 10 percent higher customer metrics, 41 percent fewer quality defects, 48 percent fewer safety accidents, and 37 percent lower employee turnover. Furthermore, business or work units that ranked in the top half of employee engagement/connection scores were twice as likely to succeed when compared to units in the bottom half (Gallup 2013a).

Skeptics argue that favorable organizational outcomes affect employee engagement more than employee engagement affects organizational outcomes. Gallup chief scientist James Harter teamed up with Frank Schmidt, the Gary C. Fethke chair in leadership and professor of management and organizations at the University of Iowa, to put this theory to the test. They and a group of researchers completed a meta-analysis on longitudinal research from 2,178 business units within 10 large organizations working in diverse industries. The research established causation by measuring across three time periods, finding conclusive evidence that engaged employees *caused* higher employee retention rates, better customer loyalty, and superior financial performance. The evidence for causality in the reverse direction—from performance to employee engagement—was, according to Schmidt, "pretty weak in comparison." The results of their study were presented in the *Perspectives on Psychological Science* article, "Causal Impact of Employee Work Perceptions on the Bottom Line of Organizations" (Harter et al. 2010).

Many other studies confirm the positive effect connection has on organizational health and performance. Here is a small sampling:

- A global research study of 50,000 individuals found that employees who feel engaged and connected are 20 percent more productive than the average employee and 87 percent less likely to leave the organization (Corporate Leadership Council 2004).

- The Hay Group (2010) studied more than 400 companies for more than seven years and found that companies with top quartile engagement and connection scores grew revenues by 2.5 to 4.5 times as much as companies with bottom quartile engagement and connection.

- A 2013 Temkin Group study of 2,400 workers in the United States found that when compared with disengaged employees, highly engaged employees are nearly six times more committed to helping their companies succeed, three times more likely to recommend improvements, and nearly five times more likely to recommend that someone apply for a job at their company.

In 1997 Arie de Geus published "The Living Company" in the *Harvard Business Review*. In it he and his team studied 27 organizations that had been in business more than 100 years, but were still important in their industries and continued to have strong corporate identities. They concluded that those companies' leaders valued the people in their organizations more than the type of tasks they performed. The study found that each of the 27 companies had changed its business portfolio at least once—chemical company DuPont began as a maker of gunpowder; Mitsui, which began as a drapery shop, also ventured into banking, mining, and manufacturing. As de Geus observed, the "case histories repeatedly show that a sense of community is essential for long-term survival" (1997).

In 2005 Google's people analytics teams began working on Project Oxygen, a multiyear study of its top-rated managers. The team used data from performance reviews, feedback surveys, and nominations from top-manager awards to identify the factors that made the best managers. The result was a list of eight leadership behaviors:

1. Be a good coach.

2. Empower your team and don't micromanage.

3. Express interest in team members' success and personal well-being.

4. Don't be a sissy: Be productive and results-oriented.

5. Be a good communicator and listen to your team.

6. Help your employees with career development.

7. Have a clear vision and strategy for the team.

8. Have technical skills so you can help advise the team.

Laszlo Bock, Google's vice president for people operations, summed up the study by saying "we'd always believed that to be a manager, particularly on the engineering side, you need to be as deep or deeper a technical expert than the people who work for you. It turns out that's absolutely the least important thing. It's important but pales in comparison. Much more important is just making that connection and being accessible" (Bryant 2011).

An understanding of connection can be enhanced by integrating research from Abraham Maslow on the hierarchy of human needs, Mihaly Csikszentmihalyi on optimal experience (or flow), Victor Frankel on meaning, and Edward L. Deci and Richard M. Ryan on autonomy. Their works, along with our research, led to the conclusion that there are six universal human needs necessary to thrive at work. The six needs, as described in chapter 1, are respect, recognition, belonging, autonomy, personal growth, and meaning. They are met when people feel connected to their work, their supervisor and colleagues, their organization's identity, and, in many cases, the people they serve (their customers, clients, or the beneficiaries of their work). The sense of connection helps them thrive. When these six needs are not met, people don't feel connected and report feeling bored, lethargic, lonely, anxious, sad, or depressed. These emotions diminish their enthusiasm and energy, which undermines their ability to perform well.

Research from the positive psychology movement also provides crucial insights into connection and how it works in organizations.

As outlined in chapter 2, the positive psychology movement identified 24 character strengths (or values) that provide a survival advantage to individuals and groups. The Character > Connection > Thrive Chain (Figure 2-1) ties all the pieces together by showing how individual character strengths (from committed members and servant leaders) promote the core elements of a connection culture (vision, value, and voice), which in turn meet the six universal human needs for individuals and organizations to thrive.

E.O. Wilson (2012), a Harvard professor and one of the world's preeminent biologists, wrote that values promoting connection among a group—including goodness, empathy, altruism, compassion, generosity, and the desire to cooperate—provide a survival advantage to groups, whereas survival is undermined by selfishness, greed, and deceit. His work challenges the view that a survival advantage accrues to species based on kin selection. Instead he argues that the evidence primarily favors group selection, and that connection is key to the group's survival, regardless of whether the members of a group are related.

## THE CURRENT STATE OF CONNECTION

Much has been written about the current state of connection, including Robert Putnam's *Bowling Alone*, David Myers' *American Paradox*, Robert Lane's *The Loss of Happiness in Market Democracies*, and, more recently, Jacqueline Olds and Richard Schwartz's *The Lonely American*. These works present compelling evidence that a broad decline in connection and community has been occurring since the post–World War II economic boom, which has contributed to a decline in both mental and physical health and life expectancy.

Thanks to modern technology and the increased pace of the modern business world, many people have less time to connect at home because they are spending more time at work or monitoring work from home via mobile devices. Some families, nuclear or extended, have chosen to spread out geographically to pursue economic opportunities, which results in less time spent connecting. Longer commute times also affect the amount of time available for connecting.

In addition to, or perhaps even because of, increased pressures at work, people are becoming more disconnected with their peers. Between 1985 and 2004, the number of Americans who said they had *not* discussed "important matters" with a friend during the prior six months tripled to nearly 25 percent of those surveyed. With fewer friends to confide in, Americans are turning to paid confidants—in 1950 Americans had a combined 33,000 paid confidants (including clinical psychologists, social workers, and therapists); by 2010 that number was estimated to be 1,091,000. However, most coaching is done for economic gain rather than personal growth and development (Marche 2012; Morris 2014).

In Western nations, physicians and nurses speak about an epidemic of loneliness, which could be due, at least in part, to increasing numbers of single-person households. In 1950, less than 10 percent of American households contained only one individual; by 2010 that number had nearly tripled to 27 percent, the highest in U.S. history (Marche 2012). From 2000 to 2010, the number of American adults over 45 who identified as being chronically lonely rose from 20 percent to 35 percent (Anderson 2010).

Other factors that may also contribute to declining connection include historically high divorce rates (which have recently been on the decline due to lower marriage rates), more two-parent working families, lower participation in community organizations including faith-based communities, higher layoffs and employee turnover, a productivity push in workplaces that has squeezed out time for people to connect in the office, and increased media use (television, online, mobile devices, gaming) that crowds out time previously spent connecting face-to-face.

## THE DANGER OF DISCONNECTION

The decline of connection increases the likelihood that organizations and individuals will be dysfunctional. When people feel disconnected, they are vulnerable to stress. And as the pace of change speeds up and competition increases in today's hyper-competitive global marketplace, stress levels will naturally rise, too. The combination of rising stress and declining psychological resources results in a volatile mix.

Short-term stress is manageable for most people, but a sustained period of stress is extremely unhealthy. During a state of stress response the human body reallocates resources, including blood, glucose, and oxygen, to bodily systems that it expects to use for fight or flight, including the heart, lungs, and thighs, while reducing those same resources to parts of the brain, digestive system, immune system, and reproductive system. If this denial of resources is sustained, it could result in feelings of ill health and even cause serious damage—after just a few hours, the lack of nutrients to the brain begins to alter the structure of neurons in the hippocampus, which is involved in the learning and memory function (Sapolsky 2010).

The combination of stress and disconnection can also trigger unhealthy behaviors. When people feel unsupported, left out, or lonely, they often turn to coping mechanisms to feel better. These behaviors run the risk of becoming obsessive and addictive because cessation produces the unpleasant sensations of withdrawal, which may include anxiety, depression, feelings of emptiness, irritability, lethargy, or numbness. Furthermore, some addictions may require increased frequency and involvement to produce the desired pleasure, causing the addictive behavior to crowd out time spent on healthy activities. People who struggle with loneliness and addictive coping behaviors are also more likely to commit suicide. In fact, suicide is now the leading cause of injury-related death in America, outnumbering even car accidents (this is similar to findings for the European Union, Canada, and China; Rocket et al. 2012).

The lack of connection has been shown to contribute to substance and process addictions. In a review of 83 studies on addiction with at least 500 subjects, Sussman et al. (2011) concluded that nearly half the adult U.S. population suffers from an addiction "with serious negative consequences." Substance additions include eating disorders as well as behaviors that attempt to manipulate pleasure by ingesting products into the body, such as dependence on alcohol, tobacco, or mood-altering legal and illegal drugs. According to Joseph Califano, head of Columbia University's Center for Alcohol and Substance Abuse (CASA), Americans account for just 4 percent of the global population, yet they consume 50 percent of the world's supply of legal mood-altering drugs and two-thirds of the world's supply of illegal drugs (CASA 2007). Process addictions are pathological behaviors that involve mood-altering events that produce feelings of pleasure. These addictions include dependence on busyness and work, exercise, shopping, gambling, gaming or social media, and love, sex, and pornography.

A lack of connection is a contributor to the alarming decline in the mental and physical health of Americans under 50. A 2013 National Research Council and Institute of Medicine report found that, in comparison to their peers in 16 wealthy nations, Americans under 50 now have the lowest average life expectancy. The report noted "when compared with the average for other high-income countries, the United States fares worse in nine health domains: adverse birth outcomes; injuries, accidents, and homicides; adolescent pregnancy and sexually transmitted infections; HIV and AIDS; drug-related mortality; obesity and diabetes; heart disease; chronic lung disease;

and disability." Loneliness has been shown to contribute to many of these adverse health outcomes. Rising stress makes the problems worse (Woolf and Aron 2014).

People in the lower end of an organization's chain of command and status hierarchy are particularly vulnerable. The pioneering Whitehall studies of British civil servants found that government workers who were lower in the hierarchy experienced poorer cardiovascular health and lower life expectancies, even though they had the same access to healthcare services as their higher-level counterparts. The researchers found that "good levels of social support had a protective effect on mental health and reduced the risk of spells of sickness absence," whereas a lack of support and unclear or inconsistent information was associated with a twofold increased risk of poor general mental health (Ferrie 2004). A more recent study found that nonleaders showed higher levels of salivary cortisol and anxiety, which are physiological and psychological indicators of stress, respectively (Sherman et al. 2012). These studies suggest that people with less power, control, influence, and status are especially in need of connection to protect them from the biological damage caused by chronic psychosocial stress and the additional damage caused by coping behaviors.

Although research on the lack of connection today is troubling, recent research showing the high priority younger generations place on connection is encouraging. When the global marketing firm McCann Worldgroup surveyed 7,000 young people (16–30-year-olds) around the world, they found that more than 90 percent rated "connection and community" as their greatest need. Younger generations long for greater connection, and leaders who engage them will create cultures that meet that need. As the researchers put it, "to truly grasp the power of connection for this generation, we can look at how they wish to be remembered. It is not for their beauty, their power, or their influence, but simply for the quality of their human relationships and their ability to look after those around them" (McCann Worldgroup 2011).

## FIVE REASONS CONNECTION CULTURES NEED TO BE A HIGH PRIORITY

This chapter argues that connection is essential, leading to greater wellness, well-being, and longer lives for individuals, and greater productivity, prosperity, and sustainability for organizations. However, in nearly all organizations, the levels of employee engagement and connection are highly dispersed (Fleming et al. 2005)—most organizations contain a mixture of connection cultures, cultures of control, and cultures of indifference, indicating that most leaders are not intentional about developing connection and connection cultures.

Drawing on research and experience, the following five reasons outline why creating connection cultures should be an organization's highest priority.

1. **Employees who feel connected perform at the top of their game.** People who feel connected experience superior wellness and well-being; are more enthusiastic, energetic, and optimistic; make better decisions; are more creative; and live longer.

2. **Employees who feel connected give their best effort.** Employees who feel connected care about achieving results, so they exert additional effort and persevere. Disconnected and disengaged employees show up for the paycheck, giving the minimum level of effort required to keep their jobs.

3. **Employees who feel connected align their behavior with organizational goals.** Research has shown that nearly one in five employees works against his or her organization's interests. However, because they care about achieving results, connected employees are more likely to work toward their supervisor's and organization's goals. Thus, organizations with greater connection experience a higher percentage of employees who pull in the same direction.

4. **Employees who feel connected help improve the quality of decisions.** Disconnected employees are less likely to give decision makers the information they need to make optimal decisions. Employees who care about their organization's performance will speak up and share that information, even if decision makers would rather not hear it.

5. **Employees who feel connected actively contribute to innovation.** Connected employees actively look for ways to improve the organization and contribute to its marketplace of ideas, which is important because innovation frequently occurs when ideas from different domains are synthesized. As a result, new products, services, processes, and businesses will arise. This cognitive process has been described as integrative thinking, blending, and connecting the dots (Martin 2007; Brooks 2011; Stallard 2007).

# 5
# TAKING ACTION: CONNECTING THROUGH VISION, VALUE, AND VOICE

---

In this chapter you will learn:

- practical actions to implement a connection culture in your organization
- why you should be aware of the knowing-doing gap.

---

Now that you've read about the who, what, where, and why, it's time for the how—how do you make a connection culture actionable and operational?

There is a broad range of practices to help create a connection culture. In the pages that follow you'll find 15 building blocks for creating and maintaining a connection culture, five each for the core connection culture elements of vision, value, and voice. While this list is not exhaustive, it will help get you started.

## VISION: INSPIRING IDENTITY THAT PRODUCES SHARED IDENTITY

*When everyone in the organization is motivated by the mission, united by the values, and proud of the reputation.*

## DEVELOP AN INSPIRATIONAL IDENTITY PHRASE THAT CONNECTS

Research shows that people who experience a sense of well-being from meaningful work exhibit gene-expression profiles that are associated with a lower risk of cancer, diabetes, and cardiovascular disease (Fredrickson et al. 2013). Connecting employees to your organization's vision, mission, or values that serve others and make a difference (also referred to as pro-social) boosts employee productivity and protects people from burnout. To increase connection, leaders must go further than simply having a vision, mission, and values by developing a brief, memorable, and inspirational identity phrase that unites people and makes them feel proud.

An identity phrase based on *vision* describes the dream of a desirable future state. Examples include MD Anderson Cancer Center's "making cancer history" and TCU's "learning to change the world."

An identity phrase based on *mission* describes a goal. Examples include Charles Schwab's mission "to provide the most useful and ethical financial products in the world," and NASA's mission during the Apollo program "to put a man on the moon by the end of the decade."

You might also consider an inspirational identity phrase based on core *values*. (Developing your core values is discussed in more detail later in this chapter.) Tata Capital's "we only do what's right for you" reflects the value of honesty, Lexus's "the relentless pursuit of perfection" reflects the values of excellence and perseverance, and Apple's "think different" and General Electric's "imagination at work" both reflect the value of creativity. To generate ideas, read through the 24 character strengths in the appendix for a list of values that inspire people.

Some organizations have more than one inspirational identity phrase. Google's mission is summed up in the phrase "to organize the world's information and make it universally accessible and useful."

The identity phrase "Don't be evil" is grounded in Google's values of fairness, honesty, and citizenship.

If your organization does not have an identity phrase, or it's time to refresh or rethink it, you could spread engagement by involving your employees. Hold a contest in which people submit inspiring identity phrases for consideration, and then have employees vote on their favorites. You'll be able to see which ones are most inspiring and make employees feel proud.

## SET THE TOP FIVE ANNUAL PRIORITIES

Both individually and as a team, set no more than five challenging but achievable annual priorities that are aligned with your mission. If you go beyond five, it will diminish connection, focus, and effective execution by overwhelming those responsible for implementation. Take time to regularly review your weekly plans to make sure they are aligned with your top five priorities.

As much as possible, let your direct reports establish their own top five annual priorities. Talk through the team's top five priorities with each employee to find shared priorities that will advance the organization's and employee's interests. It may not be possible to find a perfect set of priorities for each person, but if you make the effort you will be rewarded with people who feel more connected and execute their tasks with greater enthusiasm, energy, and effort.

## IDENTIFY AND ESTABLISH CORE VALUES THAT CONNECT

If you asked your employees what the organization's core values are, could they tell you? Most cannot. To create a connection culture, employees need to be able to articulate the organization's core values.

To identify core values that create connection, leaders should begin by taking time to reflect on the values they believe in and want to promote in their organization. Start by reflecting on your experiences, including those at and away from work, and write down any lessons you've learned from them. Then use the 24 character strengths in the appendix to reflect on what strengths are most important to you and your organization's ability to achieve its mission.

I recommend reading what other leaders have written about their core values. Starbucks CEO Howard Schultz's book *Pour Your Heart Into It* provides an excellent example. Throughout the book Schultz articulates his experiences in life, how those experiences shaped his values, and how they became the values at Starbucks. In *Fired Up or Burned Out*, I included one of the best examples I've seen of a leader concisely articulating his core values. In the Montpelier Command Philosophy, the commander of USS *Montpelier*, a nuclear submarine in the U.S. Navy, describes the values he strives to meet, which ones he expects sailors under his command to follow, and why each value is important.

After you've completed the above steps, organize your thoughts in a manner similar to the Montpelier Command Philosophy—name the value and explain why it's important. Ask trusted friends to read your values and provide feedback about what's right, wrong, or missing. Once your draft is in good shape, share it with your direct reports and ask them to provide feedback. Consider the feedback, make the changes that you believe improve it, and then circulate the revised version to your direct reports. Have them go through the feedback process with their direct reports. Continue this process until everyone on the team has had an opportunity to voice their opinions and ideas. This process creates commitment and alignment with core values.

Finally, take your direct reports through the final core values you decide upon. Discuss and identify which values are most important to your team's success, which values your team is strong in, which values it needs to develop, and what can be done to develop and live by each value. Follow up with a written summary of your plan to "live our values." It should include action items, responsibilities, and due dates.

## CONTINUOUSLY RECONNECT PEOPLE TO YOUR INSPIRING IDENTITY

Connection to an organization's identity diminishes over time, so look for ways to keep people connected to your vision, mission, and values. Consider taking employees to visit customers, or bring customers in to talk with employees about how they use and benefit from the products and services. Circulate any press materials about your organization that reinforce your mission, values, and reputation.

Hold "continuous improvement" meetings three to four times a year to identify innovative ways to improve and achieve your mission. These meetings could be focused on ways to increase revenue, reduce costs, improve quality, or improve efficiency. List the ideas, prioritize them, select a manageable set to focus on, assign responsibilities, and track their completion. Make this information available to the entire group. Such meetings get people thinking proactively about how to improve.

You should also meet periodically with your direct reports to review and revise your plan to live out the core values; ask your direct reports to do the same with their direct reports. Consider having your core values printed on a small card that can fit in a wallet. Each Ritz-Carlton employee receives a card with the organization's core values (called Ritz Basics) printed on the front and back. Teams meet briefly every day to review one of the 20 Ritz Basics, and each week the company highlights a Ritz-Carlton employee who lived out a value.

Don't forget to celebrate your successes. When your team accomplishes a major goal that helps achieve your mission, celebrate with a party, meal, or outing. Ask people for suggestions about how to celebrate, and if you can afford it, invite them to bring a significant other to join in.

Celebrate culture carriers who embody your culture because they contribute to achieving your mission while behaving in ways that are consistent with your organization's values. Create a blog or book to share stories about these people and their practices; see the annual *Culture Book* from Zappos or *Smile Guide: Employee Perspectives on Culture, Loyalty, and Profit* from Beryl Companies for examples. You can also have your employees provide positive examples, and establish a rewards and recognition program. These actions encourage everyone to become culture carriers.

## HIRE, DEVELOP, AND PROMOTE FOR COMPETENCE AND CONNECTION SKILLS

Most managers hire and promote for competence, but are not as intentional about assessing connection skills. Involve many individuals in your organization's hiring and promotion processes. Have them compare notes by taking into consideration your organization's values and the 24 character strengths before making hiring and promotion recommendations.

New employee orientation and new leader training must also address connection. Creating a connection culture requires developing a certain mindset in leaders. Education is essential. In order to gain the support of your leaders, they must understand what a connection culture is, why it's important, and how they can create and sustain it. This information must be communicated to all current leaders during leadership training sessions and incorporated into new leader orientation.

People need to be encouraged and inspired to think of themselves as both committed members and servant leaders. To do this, leadership training should include inspiring stories that celebrate committed members and servant leaders and describe how they contribute to connection culture. This will encourage people to develop their own character strengths and connect. The inspiring stories presented in chapter 3 are excellent examples.

When educating your employees, remember to teach new terminology, including the definitions and descriptions of connection,

connection culture, cultures of control, cultures of indifference, vision, value, voice, committed members, and servant leaders. They also need to learn about important frameworks that help to develop mental models and guide behavior, such as the connection culture model and the Character > Connection > Thrive Chain. Presenting leaders with applicable research studies is another way to support a rational argument. Finally, creating a successful connection culture depends on whether or not practices that connect are acted upon by each individual. The practices must be taught, serving to both educate people and help them become intentional.

Providing a good variety of content in training makes it easier to reach people regardless of their learning style. Left-brain-oriented engineers and scientists, for example, will be most receptive to research and hard data, whereas right-brain-oriented creative personalities will be more drawn to visual diagrams, stories, and case studies.

Implement an employee engagement and connection survey to provide accountability. Most leaders are mistaken in their assessment of the engagement and connection of people they lead. As a result, they don't recognize an employee engagement problem until they feel the pain from underperformance or face reality in the form of poor results from an employee engagement and connection survey. The survey should ask all employees how their team, department, and organization are doing when it comes to acting in ways that are consistent with your organization's values.

Surveys can be designed to pinpoint where the organization's values are being met and where connection cultures, cultures of control, and cultures of indifference are found within an organization. It is typical to have a mix of subcultures when organizations do not intentionally develop culture. While some outstanding senior leaders are able to rely on interactions with people (rather than surveys) to identify pockets of disconnection throughout the organization, it is rare to find a leader who has the time to do this well. Conducting employee engagement and connection surveys on an annual basis is a best practice that provides a systematic way to assess connection and hold leaders responsible for creating connection cultures.

The vast majority of managers who don't take the time to connect with the people they are responsible for leading do so because they don't see a clear link between behaviors that connect and superior performance results. One way to demonstrate that link is to integrate employee engagement and connection survey data with operational and financial metrics to show leaders how greater connection leads to superior performance and results. This gets their attention and encourages them to improve employee engagement and connection by creating connection cultures.

Assessing connection both within and between organizational units, where interconnection, interaction, and cooperation are critical to achieve results, is highly recommended. For example, connections should be assessed between sales and marketing departments, between sales and customer service departments, and between support functions and the departments they support. When interdepartmental connections are broken, it affects employee engagement as well as results.

Employee engagement and connection surveys also help identify servant leaders and committed members who can be emulated. Celebrating these individuals and groups through organizational communications (such as the company intranet, social media, and print publications) sends a powerful message and promotes best practices. This is particularly important because research has shown that standard practices within a culture have a higher probability of adoption (Dorsey 2000).

Finally, surveys hold leaders accountable so that connection cultures are maintained. They recognize leaders who are good at creating connection cultures and provide an important early warning system to help identify leaders and units that have drifted away from connection cultures. In time, a decision may need to be made whether or not a leader is capable of working within a connection culture or should be replaced. Leaders with strengths in connection can become peer mentors to those who are struggling.

## VALUE: HUMAN VALUE THAT PRODUCES SHARED EMPATHY

*When everyone in the organization understands the needs of people, appreciates their positive unique contributions, and helps them achieve their potential.*

### GET PEOPLE IN THE RIGHT ROLE

Most leaders identify the roles and responsibilities of people who can help achieve their organization's mission. To increase connection, leaders must help the people they lead get into roles that fit their interests and strengths, and provide the right degree of challenge. If leaders can't get people in the ideal role, they should at least try to assign them responsibilities or projects that fit them well. Achieving alignment with employee competence, connection skills, and the requirements of a particular job should take place in both hiring and promotion decisions.

To learn about the interests of your employees, take time to get to know them. Ask questions to learn about their lives and what's important to them, such as, "What are you passionate about?" "How do you like to work?" and "Which leaders have inspired you and why?" Ask what they liked and didn't like about their prior work experiences. Find out what their career aspirations are. These questions provide insight into how employees are wired, including what they value. Write down what you learn and identify specific actions you can take to get them in the right role and help them make progress toward their aspirations.

## CREATE PERSONAL DEVELOPMENT PLANS

People are more engaged and feel more connected when they are learning, growing, and experiencing a sense of progress. Work with your direct reports to create personal development plans addressing areas that require growth in order to achieve their potential. Help them make wise goals to advance their careers, and put steps in place to help them achieve these goals. To evaluate progress and provide feedback, establish objective, quantifiable benchmarks whenever possible. Doing so will boost their effectiveness and connection to you.

When providing feedback to help someone improve, communicate in private whenever possible, be respectful in your tone of voice and volume, and begin with three positive traits you like about that person's work or character. After sharing the three positives, say, "I believe you would be even better if . . . [insert what you want him to do or stop doing]." Kindness matters and the approach you take will affect how the person receives the feedback.

## PROVIDE TRAINING AND MENTORS TO SUPPORT PERSONAL DEVELOPMENT

Do you ever wonder why all world-class athletes have coaches? It's because no one becomes great at anything that requires skill unless they undergo training and have coaches or mentors who help them grow. We all have blind spots—actions that are disconnecting—and we need coaches and mentors to help us see them and then advise, encourage, and hold us accountable so that we grow to become intentional connectors.

To support personal development, provide training and mentors. It would be beneficial to provide mentor training to all supervisors. Make peer mentors available for any direct reports who want to improve in a specific area of competence or character, and select a mentor who is strong in the given area. One way to match mentors and mentees is to use a flash mentoring format, which asks participants to commit to meeting once to see if both parties connect, and if the mentor has the knowledge, expertise, and time available to meet the mentee's needs and expectations. If both parties agree to continue, they should set a finite number of additional meetings, rather than leave the term open-ended. Unless both mentor and mentee agree to the arrangement, there is no commitment to meet again (Derrick and Wooley 2009).

Larger organizations should implement integrated leader training and development. For example, Yale New Haven Health System (YNHHS) develops leaders using a combination of high-quality classroom instruction, coaching, mentoring, workplace application, and senior leadership involvement. YNHHS creates cohorts of high-potential directors and vice presidents from across its system of hospitals (for example, six nurses, three physicians, and six administrators) who complete the six-month program together. The program uses a 70-20-10 model: 70 percent of the learning comes from workplace application and working in teams on systemwide projects that apply new skills, 20 percent comes from coaching and mentoring, and 10 percent comes from classroom instruction. It also includes an assessment of each participant's leadership competencies and character values. Results have been impressive. The program developed interpersonal, interdepartmental, and intersystem relationships (connections) across YNHHS hospitals, and out of a recent cohort of 15 participants, 10 (67 percent) were promoted and all were given expanded responsibilities.

## HELP PEOPLE DEVELOP CONNECTION SKILLS

Everyone in your organization needs to develop connection skills, especially leaders. Managers lead from authority, whereas leaders lead from a combination of authority and connection. It is not unusual for managers who are good at organizing tasks to require help developing the personal leadership skills necessary to better connect and maintain a connection with people. Weak connection skills hold many managers back from becoming leaders that people want to follow. The following attitudes, language, and behaviors will help facilitate connection.

*Recognize varying connection needs.* People have different predispositions when it comes to their sensitivities to feeling connection or lack thereof. People also respond differently to actions in terms of whether or not it makes them feel connected. Learn about the people you lead, and tailor your behaviors to connect based on what you've learned about each individual.

*Be present in conversations.* It has been said that attention is oxygen for relationships. When meeting with people, get in the habit of being present by giving them your full attention. Show that you are engaged and interested by asking questions, and then asking follow-up questions to clarify. Listen carefully, observing facial expressions and body cues. Don't break the connection by checking your phone, looking around the room, or letting your mind wander.

*Develop the ability to empathize.* Mutual empathy is a powerful connector that is made possible by mirror neurons in our brains. Mirror neurons act like an emotional Wi-Fi system (Goleman 2006). When we feel the emotions of others, it makes them feel connected to us. When we feel their positive emotion, it enhances the positive emotion they feel. When we feel their pain, it diminishes the pain they feel. If someone expresses emotion, it's OK, and natural, for you to feel it too.

*Develop the habit of emphasizing positives.* Psychologist John Gottman (1994) first observed that marriages were less likely to survive when the positive/negative ratio of interactions dipped below 5-to-1 (or five positive interactions to every negative interaction). More recently, psychologist Barbara Fredrickson (2002) found that a positivity ratio also applied in the workplace. People need affirmation and recognition, so get in the habit of looking for ways to affirm and serve others. Do this by looking for task strengths and character strengths, which reflect the excellence of a person's work and the way that person goes about her work, respectively. For example, you might affirm a colleague by saying, "Nancy, that was an outstanding website you created. The navigation design was easy to use, the writing was easy to understand, and the color scheme was beautiful." You might affirm her character strengths by saying, "Nancy, I appreciate the way you persevered to make our new website happen. You showed wisdom and humility in seeking the ideas of others and applying the best ideas to the design of our new website. Very nicely done."

*Control your tone of voice.* Recognize that people will instinctively react to the delivery of your message before they hear its content. They may put up a wall and become defensive or feel threatened if your tone of voice is booming, shrill, or strident.

*Negotiate with the mindset to solve a problem rather than to win.* You can build connections with people during negotiations if you adopt and maintain the right mindset. Thinking of the people you are negotiating with as competitors leads to disconnection and distrust. Instead, think of them as holding knowledge that you need in order to identify a win-win solution. Negotiating requires probing, patience, and perseverance to understand other people's objectives, perceptions, and sensitivities.

*Provide autonomy in execution.* Monitor progress and be available to help your direct reports, but refrain from micromanaging unless they ask for specific help. Favor guidelines rather than rules and controls, and let people know that you are available if they have questions or would like you to act as a sounding board. This meets the human need for autonomy and allows people to experience personal growth.

*Learn and apply the five languages of appreciation.* Ask your direct reports about the times they remember receiving recognition at work. Find out what their primary and secondary languages of appreciation are. The five languages of appreciation in the workplace are words of affirmation, quality time, acts of service, gifts, and physical touch. However, note that physical touch is not a primary language of appreciation in the workplace, and should generally be avoided. To learn more, read Gary Chapman and Paul White's *The 5 Languages of Appreciation in the Workplace*.

*Apologize when you make a mistake.* We all make mistakes, but not everyone says they're sorry. Apologizing is an important step that will help rebuild connection.

*Develop social skills and relationship skills, and recognize the difference between them.* Many individuals develop social skills, which make them excellent networkers who impress and connect with others in casual interactions. However, in addition to social skills, it is essential to develop relationship skills, which help create deeper connections with a few people who have your back. Consider the skills you use when meeting someone for the first time versus nurturing your relationship with a best friend. Relationship skills— regularly spending time with an individual, being open to sharing your struggles, sharing someone's joy and pain, being there in times of need, and so on—help develop the deeper connections that are necessary for individual wellness and well-being to thrive in life and achieve sustainable superior performance.

## MAKE CONNECTIONS THAT ARE PERSONAL

Take time to connect with people on a personal level. Resist the inclination to skip time spent in conversation getting to know the people you lead. This is an important step. Psychologist James Pennebaker (1997) has found that when you get people to talk, they feel more connected to you, like you more, and believe they learn more from you. Meet with your employees over a meal or coffee, and ask questions that are unrelated to work, such as "Where were you born?" "What are your interests outside of work?" or "What are you looking forward to in the future?"

Leaders should schedule regular social time for people to connect. Genentech has a weekly Friday afternoon social time where they serve drinks and snacks. I know a manager who orders pizza and salad for his team every other Friday. During the warm summer months, organize an ice cream social to bring your team together for conversation. Consider helping serve those in attendance, and make sure to say hello to everyone. Avoid talking about work; instead ask people about their interests or what they are looking forward to during the remainder of the year.

## VOICE: KNOWLEDGE FLOW THAT PRODUCES SHARED UNDERSTANDING

*When everyone in the organization seeks the ideas of others, shares their ideas and opinions honestly, and safeguards relational connections.*

### CREATE FORUMS FOR ORGANIZATION-WIDE COMMUNICATION

Hold meetings periodically that bring everyone you lead together to discuss how you are making progress toward achieving your mission. In addition, communicate the opportunities and challenges your organization is facing and how you plan to address them. The meetings should address progress in quantitative, measurable terms, while also connecting the mission to how it serves others and brings greater beauty, goodness, or truth to the world. Include stories that show how your organization is achieving its mission.

Make time for questions and answers at the meeting, or in separate meetings to give people a voice. You can have people anonymously submit questions ahead of time or simply ask them during the meeting. Howard Behar, former president of Starbucks North America and Starbucks International, called the sessions he held "Open Forums." Jim Goodnight, CEO of SAS Institute, holds "Java with Jim" sessions. Vineet Nayar, CEO of HCL Technologies, has people email questions, which he answers on his blog so everyone can see the question and his response. The founders of Google also do this at each Friday's TGIF meeting.

During meetings, be sure to listen actively. Jane Dutton, professor of business administration and psychology of the University of Michigan, has several suggestions. For example, you might paraphrase by expressing what you heard in your own words ("Let me make sure I'm hearing you correctly. You are saying . . . ") or summarize what you heard ("Let me summarize your points to see if I fully understand. I hear you saying . . . "). A third approach is to clarify by asking questions ("Tell me if I'm hearing you correctly. I think you are saying . . . ").

## HOLD KNOWLEDGE FLOW SESSIONS FOR DECISION INPUT AND IDEA DEVELOPMENT

Holding knowledge flow sessions is a practice that promotes connection through open communications—listening to others' opinions and ideas then considering them before making decisions. Team knowledge flow sessions should occur regularly to keep the team aligned and accountable (one organization I know calls their weekly operational knowledge flow session the "Sweat the Details" meeting). You may also want to hold a skip-level knowledge flow session periodically, in which you meet with a direct report and his direct reports.

Begin meetings with positive comments to boost energy and creativity. Share your vision—your thoughts about what actions need to be done, by whom, and when each action needs to be completed.

Make sure to ask people who are quiet to share what they think. Listen and consider the ideas put forth and implement good ideas, giving credit where it's due. This practice reflects the character strengths of integrity, humility, curiosity, and open-mindedness.

In addition to group knowledge flow sessions, you can hold one-to-one knowledge flow sessions. Begin by making a list of the people you interact with in order to perform your work well. When meeting with individuals, share your vision for what relevant actions need to be taken in your work, whom you see as responsible for each action, and when it needs to be completed. Ask them to tell you what's right, what's wrong, and what's missing from your thinking, and consider their ideas and opinions to learn from them and show you value them. After each group or individual knowledge flow session, follow up in writing to summarize what you heard, what actions are necessary, who is responsible for each action, and when each action should be completed.

## MAINTAIN STAFF CONNECTION AND DEVELOPMENT

Strong relationships are maintained by staying in touch. British prime minister Winston Churchill understood this. Historians have found more than 1,700 letters, notes, and telegrams that Churchill wrote to his wife so that they would remain connected. Take a page from Churchill's playbook. Stay connected with your direct reports by meeting weekly with them in person, if at all possible. If you cannot meet weekly, use check-ins—phone calls, emails, and text messages—to help you stay connected. For people who work remotely, regularly call or Skype with them. Remote work can be lonely and people should believe that you are on their team and want to help them achieve their potential. In addition to work issues, ask about how they are doing personally. There is much truth to the old saying that people don't care what you know until they know you care.

The deepest connections are formed when you are open to communicate who you really are, what you really believe, and your struggles in life. Consider sharing lessons you've learned from past mistakes if it will help another person. This openness communicates humility and promotes connection and trust. If you are uncertain about when it is appropriate to be open in a particular context, seek the advice of trusted friends.

Encourage other people to tell their stories, too. Have you ever asked how someone's day went only to hear the standard reply, "fine"? If you really want to connect, try saying, "I would really like to know how your day went, so tell me stories." This practice also works well with children, spouses, and friends.

You might also consider having your team periodically read a book together. Select a business book for your direct reports or team members to read, then meet to identify any themes or ideas that you could implement. Visit www.ConnectionCulture.com for book recommendations.

## CONDUCT KNOWLEDGE FLOW SESSIONS TO EVALUATE EVENTS AND ACTIVITIES

Every completed event provides an opportunity for learning and improvement. Post-event knowledge flow evaluation sessions give people an opportunity to identify what went right, what went wrong, and what was missing. This practice gives people a voice and helps make continuous improvements.

One type of knowledge flow session for evaluation is the stop-start-continue meeting to review your team's activities. Identify any activities your team should start that they are not presently doing, current activities they should stop doing, and activities they should continue doing.

## PROVIDE TRAINING TO SAFEGUARD RELATIONAL CONNECTIONS

Communicate that constructive friction is desirable. People will often have differences of opinion, and leaders should assure them that it is healthy. With this understanding, holding and voicing opposing views shouldn't grow into combat. The key to maintaining healthy constructive friction is to make sure you are trying to "get it right" to promote task excellence, rather than "be right" for the purpose of personal pride. Furthermore, civility should be encouraged, especially as individuals work through their differences.

Remind your employees to safeguard relational connections, and avoid attacking people who disagree with them. If you disagree with someone, say so, but do it in a respectful manner. You could begin your response with, "I may be wrong, but is it possible that . . ?" or "It's just one person's opinion, but I believe that . . . " If you offended or hurt someone's feelings, apologize. If people apologize to you, give them the benefit of the doubt and forgive them.

Author and executive coach Marshall Goldsmith recommends that when someone offers an idea, suggestion, opinion, or plan, you should take the time to reflect before offering a suggestion to improve it. Many people are in the habit of quickly adding their better idea by saying "but" or "however." Habitually doing this undermines connection, commitment, and engagement. People implement their own ideas with greater enthusiasm and energy, so consider whether your enhancement really matters before offering it.

---

By implementing the actions in these 15 building blocks you will create and maintain a connection culture and avoid the very real risk that cultures of control and cultures of indifference will sabotage your performance. Beware the *knowing-doing gap*, a term coined by Stanford professors Jeffrey Pfeffer and Robert Sutton that recognizes many leaders get stuck in the smart talk trap when they fail to turn knowledge into actions that produce measurable results.

To make an intentional commitment to creating and maintaining your connection culture, you might want to establish a culture committee, office, or center to promote a connection culture across interdependent groups (such as groups within an organization that are dependent on each other to perform well). Southwest Airlines' culture services department has 31 full-time employees, including eight culture ambassadors who are embedded within different operational departments. Furthermore, the company's 160 culture committee members are spread throughout the organization. Southwest's culture services department collects stories that celebrate employees who live out the company's values, and post two to three on its intranet each business day.

Whether you're able to implement all 15 building blocks or only three, the most important thing is to do what you can. Don't worry if you can't do all of them immediately—it's perfectly fine to start small and work up from there. With each effort you and your team make, you gain momentum. Most importantly, implementing steps to build a connection culture ultimately creates a competitive advantage for you, your team, and your company. So get started!

# 6

# WHOM WILL YOU CHOOSE TO BECOME?

In this chapter you will learn:

- the leadership qualities needed to transform workplace cultures
- how you can personally influence local cultures in your workplace.

For individuals and organizations to thrive from the benefits of connection, the leader of the future needs to look much different than the stereotypical leader of the present. There are three types of people when it comes to connection. Which are you?

The first type is the intentional disconnector. Psychologists describe these men and women as members of the Dark Triad: psychopaths, narcissists, and Machiavellians. They lack empathy and, as a result, are unable to feel the emotions of others. They are focused on themselves and don't value others. Although they often learn how to manipulate others for awhile and can appear smooth and charming, over time people see through them and discover that they are unable to connect.

The second type is the unintentional disconnector. This represents most of us. We have blind spots that hold us back in our ability to consistently connect with others. There are many types of blind spots, including being a know-it-all, being argumentative, and being a people pleaser who doesn't speak honestly when it's uncomfortable to say what you believe. If we don't become intentional about dealing with habits that hinder connection, they will become deeply ingrained in our character.

If, however, you are intentional about seeking the feedback of others and working to develop new and better habits of connection, you can join the ranks of the third type of person: the intentional connector. The leaders we praise in this book are intentional connectors. Their leadership has enhanced the performance of the organization and the lives of the people they've served, including the employees and customers.

## TO INFINITY AND BEYOND

At the first of 2009's four smaller Academy Awards ceremonies, the Associated Press reported that it wasn't the host, actress Jessica Biel, who attracted the most attention. Instead, it was an understated, bespectacled computer engineer named Ed Catmull. When his name was announced to receive an Oscar for his lifetime of work in computer animation, the crowd went wild, whistling and whooping. The influence Catmull and his collaborators have had on Hollywood may last for decades to come, if not forever.

Catmull, the president of Pixar Animation and Walt Disney Animation Studios, formed Pixar in response to the disconnection that is the norm in Hollywood and Silicon Valley, where independent contractors come together for a specific project and then disband upon the project's conclusion. In contrast to the independent contractor model, Pixar keeps the team together so that they build connection.

Catmull has described Pixar's culture this way: "[Pixar has] an environment that nurtures trusting and respectful *relationships* and unleashes everyone's creativity. . . . The result is a vibrant community where talented people are loyal to one another and their collective work, everyone feels that they are part of something extraordinary, and their passion and accomplishments make the community a magnet for talented people" (Catmull 2008; emphasis added).

What sets Pixar apart is its intentionality about creating a culture that fuels connection and creativity. In most organizations only 25 percent of employees—the managers and the stars—feel connected to their organization. At Pixar, the percentage of employees who feel connected is much higher.

Typically, an overwhelming majority of employees feel that senior management does not value their contributions. Not so at Pixar. Catmull says that great movies are made from the "tens of thousands of ideas" that go into them from beginning to completion. As such, everyone needs to contribute their ideas and opinions, everyone's work matters, and everyone makes a difference in the quality of a film. He also emphasizes that the environment must be safe to tell the truth. Thus, it is not surprising that Pixar employees are so engaged. And because they are more engaged, Pixar employees put more effort into their work, are more trusting, and are more cooperative—all factors that affect productivity, quality, and innovation.

Contributing to connection across the organization is Pixar University, the in-house professional development and employee education program that offers courses related to filmmaking, the arts, health, and other topics of interest to Pixar employees, who can take up to four hours of classes each week. In class, participants develop acquaintances across the firm, further strengthening their ties to the organization. Pixar University's crest bears the Latin phrase *alienus non dieutius*, which means "alone no longer."

Who leaders *are* is just as important, perhaps even more so, than what they *do*. For Ed Catmull, "inclusive" is not mere rhetoric or the occasional action. He deeply believes in it, and John Lasseter, Pixar and Disney Animation Studio CEO, does too. They, in turn, select leaders who embrace these values, such as the team of director Brad Bird and producer John Walker (who worked together on *The Incredibles*).

Some years ago, I met with John Walker at Pixar's headquarters in Emeryville, California. Listening to Walker, it was clear that he embodies the values of connection. He has the sort of bridge-building personality that helps people amicably resolve conflict and keep them feeling like a part of the community. During the course of our conversation, Walker told me how he gathers the entire team working on a movie (anywhere from 200 to 300 people) at least once a week so that the extroverted artists and their more introverted technical counterparts can come together as a community. In the meetings, everyone is informed about the film's progress and encouraged to think about how to solve the present set of issues facing the team.

Catmull says his focus on culture is a "day-in, day-out full-time job." In his book *Creativity Inc.* Catmull writes about a time he missed something that threatened Pixar. Following the release of *Toy Story*, several production managers no longer wanted to work at Pixar. Although they were proud of the film, they said they felt disrespected and treated like second-class citizens by the creative department. Catmull was stunned. After all, his door was always open. He preached that everyone should be respected and have a voice. He walked the talk. How could he have missed this? Why didn't they say something earlier?

With additional investigation, Catmull discovered that the artists in the creative department, as well as the technical staff, viewed the production managers as micromanagers and obstacles to creating great animated films. As it turned out, the production managers were requiring all communications to go through the chain of command. This created a knowledge trap, which is a source of disconnection based on relationship failure. (Knowledge traps can arise from internal rivalries, silo behavior, decision makers who lack the humility to seek and consider ideas and opinions of others, and isolationist behavior.) At Pixar, the creative and technical departments were reacting to the sub-culture of control created by production managers.

To fix the situation, Catmull and Lasseter gathered the employees and made it clear that going forward decisions needed to respect the chain of command. However "anyone should be able to talk to anyone else, at any level, at any time, without fear of reprimand. . . . People talking directly to one another then letting the manager find out later was more efficient than trying to make sure that everything happened in the 'right' order and through the 'proper' channels" (Catmull 2014).

Although it took time for people to adjust to more open communications, by the time Pixar completed *A Bug's Life*, the production managers were viewed and treated as first-class citizens. They felt connected. With the change, "we had become better," said Catmull.

In 2006, Disney bought Pixar to boost its struggling Walt Disney Animation Studios unit and to help improve the culture. Catmull and Lasseter were appointed to lead the unit as president and CEO, respectively. At Disney, they discovered a culture where the creative people were not valued and felt disconnected. With encouragement from Catmull and Lasseter, the Disney Animation leaders created a culture where everyone felt connected, especially in the areas of value and voice. After the change, Disney began producing hits, such as *Tangled* and *Wreck It Ralph*. If any doubt existed that the Disney magic was back, it was shattered with the 2013 release of the Oscar-winning blockbuster *Frozen*. Having earned well more than a billion dollars in revenue at the box office in its first six months, *Frozen* became the highest-grossing animated feature ever and became one of the top-10 worldwide highest grossing movies of all time.

# MUST A CONNECTION CULTURE START AT THE TOP?

Does culture have to come from the top of the organization? That would be the ideal situation, but if the leaders at the top of your organization are not intentional about creating a connection culture, there is still hope.

Most organizations have a mix of cultures that include connection cultures, cultures of control, and cultures of indifference. Although the macro-culture of your overall organization will influence your local culture, it does not determine it. The primary determinant of connection for you is the attitude, language, and behavior of those in your local culture. For that reason, you can have an influence on your local culture, especially if you are a leader (formal or informal) at that level. I frequently see leaders change their local culture for the better.

Several years ago, one of my clients, FCB, a leading global advertising network, hired a leader to manage its New Zealand agency, which had approximately 60 employees and was lagging in the marketplace. The new leader boosted vision by expanding the local leadership team and asking them to work together to create the culture they always wanted to work in. He boosted value by being approachable and getting to know all the people in the agency. When the global financial crisis affected the agency shortly after he arrived, rather than laying people off and imposing compulsory salary reductions on frontline staff like competitors had, he challenged the leadership team to make its top priority to save as many jobs as possible. He asked the executive team leaders to join him in taking a 10 percent pay cut, which they did. He boosted voice by putting an annual employee engagement survey in place and acting on the employees' feedback. He also shared financials with employees and asked them to help find ways to reduce costs in order to save jobs. The empowered employees found ways to cut costs and, as a result, they didn't have to cut any jobs.

Pulling through tough times brought the agency together. Today FCB New Zealand is consistently recognized as one of the best places to work and the best company in its marketplace. It's won global recognition for creativity and has grown to almost four times its original size. Acknowledged as one of the best industry leaders in the Asia-Pacific region, the leader of FCB New Zealand was recently appointed vice chairman of the overall global organization, in recognition of his quick turnaround of the business, remarkable results, and superior leadership.

## CONNECTION BEGINS WITH YOU

There are people who know they need more connection, yet fail to act, which they eventually regret. Don't let that become your story. Be intentional about developing the habits of attitude, language, and behavior that connect, and work to develop a connection culture in your organization. Start local and see how it grows from there. This book has given you the tools and guidance you need to take action.

As you become an intentional connector at work, look at how the level of connection in your personal life changes. Keep the formula Vision + Value + Voice = Connection in mind and consider how it applies to your family, your neighborhood, the community organizations you are involved in, and other areas of your life, and then take action to increase connection in those spheres as well. Be intentional about developing your character strengths.

Mark this day—begin connecting and watch what happens. I promise that over time, you will see that connection affects much more than the bottom line. As you experience greater peace, hope, and joy that comes from having an abundance of connection in your life, you will discover wealth of even greater value.

# ACKNOWLEDGMENTS

I grew up in a family of boys living in a neighborhood of boys. Our lives revolved around the rhythm of three seasons: baseball, basketball, and football. Like many boys, we were not all that emotionally or socially intelligent. What I learned about connection and the emotions that increase connection, such as love and affection, came primarily from my devoted mother, Dorothy Hufstedler. Mom, for your loving influence and example, I am immensely grateful.

As an adult, I got caught up in the pursuit of money, power, and status, and that drive increasingly crowded out relationships. It was only later in life that I learned (the hard way) that we are hardwired to connect. I thank God, my family, and friends for saving me from myself. To Katie Stallard, my best friend, wife, and colleague, and our daughters, Sarah and Elizabeth, each of you has had a profound effect on me when it comes to experiencing and understanding connection, and healing from the damage of disconnection. I am so very blessed and grateful that we are a family and that our extended family is deeply connected.

To God and my church family, thank you for being and modeling connection. To my men's Bible study, I'm so thankful that we are connected by going through life together and being there for one another during the joys and challenges.

Finally, thank you to the many individuals who have helped make *Connection Culture* possible or contributed their talents to making it better. At E Pluribus Partners, thank you Katie Stallard, Jason Pankau, Carolyn Dewing-Hommes, Mitch Dickey, and Katie Russell. Katie is an exemplar of connection and character. She is my sounding board, editor, and encourager. Jason and I have been friends working together for more than a decade. He is a source of wisdom and someone I can always count on. Along with Jason, Carolyn was instrumental in the early days of putting language around the core elements of a connection culture. Mitch's ideas have influenced me, particularly his insights about how tasks and relationships produce results and how connection relates to power. Katie Russell contributed to the manuscript while ably leading our communications and social media efforts. At ATD, I would like to thank Ron Lippock, Melissa Jones, Angela Leppig, Alicia Cipriani, Julia Liapidova, and Jenna Smith. Ron leads ATD's Management Community of Practice and advocated for *Connection Culture*. Melissa, our editor at ATD Press, went above and beyond to make the book even better.

Many people at TCU have supported and contributed to our work, including Victor Boschini, Dee Dodson, Nowell Donovan, Homer Erekson, Angela Kaufman, Ann Louden, Karyn Purvis, Tracy Syler-Jones, Amanda Nickerson, and Chris Sawyer.

Finally, thank you to the many family, friends, and others who contributed ideas, feedback, or other support for *Connection Culture*, including Janis Apted, Cindy Augustine, Mary Jo Asmus, Bob Beaudine, Howard Behar, Jeff Benner, Hillary Bercovici, Jim Blasingame, Wally Bock, Bart Breen, Holly Brittingham, S. Max Brown, Anita Bruzzese, Rob and Beth Bull, David Burkus, Karen Christensen, Vernon and Connie Clark, Peter Clayton, Tom Cole, Jack Covert, Bryan Crawford, Mike and Jeannie Cunnion, Holly Dahlman, Steve Daniel, James daSilva, Joe and Lucille D'Auria, Robbie de Villiers, Kevin Eikenberry, Mary Esser, Josh Estrada, George Faller, Pat Farnack, Michael Fitzgerald, Mark Fortier and Pamela Peterson from Fortier PR, J. Theodore George, Phil Gerbyshak, Christi Gibson, Paula Godar, Seth Godin, Marshall Goldsmith, Scott Greenlee, Sally Haldorson, Arnie Herz, Lisa Haneberg, John and Bunny Harrison, Lindsey Hall, Frances Hesselbein, Johannes and Tabea Hettig, William J. Holstein, Russ Hufstedler, Matt Hultquist, Shawn Hunter, Michael

Hyatt, Prakash Idnani, Nathan Ives, Guy Kawasaki, David Kelly, Jessica Kensek, Angela Killian, Alexander Kjerulf, Jeremie Kubicek, Terry and Leslie Laughren, Jim Lemler, Chip Lewis, Mark Linsz, Thomas Loarie, Rick Lyons, Drew Marshall, Greg Marshall, Roger Martin, Dan McCarthy, Mary Beth McEuen, Shawn McEvoy, Michael McKinney, Denise McMahan, Michael Meek, Dwayne Melancon, Paul and Lisa Michalski, Morgan Mitchell, Cecile Morgan, Jay Morris, Robert Morris, Jenifer Morrison, Don Pape, John Pearson, Colton Perry, Gordon Peters, Jon Peters, Henry and Barbara Price, Becky Powell-Schwartz, Steve Roesler, Francis Rose, Bruce Rosenstein, Kris Rutledge, George Ryerson, Zane Safrit, Tim Sanders, Roy Saunderson, Rosa Say, Dan Schawbel, Beth Schelske, Aaron Schleicher, Dylan Schleicher, Terrence Seamon, John Seel, Rajesh Setty, Ken Shelton, Joshua Simpson, Katherine Snedeker, Mark Spear, Joe Stallard, Susan Stamm, Michael Bungay Stanier, Tara Stevens, Mark Thompson, Khiem and Vicki Ting, Wayne Turmel, Joe Tye, Bob Varney, Alana Weiss, Paul White, Drew Williams, Christopher Winters, Sean Witty, Heather Wright, John Young, Susan Zeidman, and David Zinger.

# APPENDIX I:
# VIA INSTITUTE
# CLASSIFICATION OF
# CHARACTER STRENGTHS

The following are descriptions of the 24 character strengths. Based on the findings of positive psychology, the character strengths were developed by the VIA Institute on Character, a not-for-profit organization focused on advancing both the science and practice of character strengths. (Note that here the 24 character strengths are organized into six virtue categories, rather than into vision, value, and voice, as we organized them to show how they support a connection culture.)

## THE CLASSIFICATION OF CHARACTER STRENGTHS

1. **Wisdom and knowledge:** Cognitive strengths that entail the acquisition and use of knowledge.

   ◦ **Creativity** (originality, ingenuity): Thinking of novel and productive ways to conceptualize and do things; includes artistic achievement but is not limited to it.

   ◦ **Curiosity** (interest, novelty-seeking, openness to experience): Taking an interest in ongoing experience for its own sake; finding subjects and topics fascinating; exploring and discovering.

   ◦ **Judgment** (open-mindedness; critical thinking): Thinking things through and examining them from all sides; not jumping to conclusions; being able to change one's mind in light of evidence; weighing all evidence fairly.

- **Love of Learning:** Mastering new skills, topics, and bodies of knowledge, whether on one's own or formally; related to the strength of curiosity but goes beyond it to describe the tendency to add systematically to what one knows.

- **Perspective** (wisdom): Being able to provide wise counsel to others; having ways of looking at the world that make sense to oneself or others.

2. **Courage:** Emotional strengths that involve the exercise of will to accomplish goals in the face of external or internal opposition.

- **Bravery** (valor): Not shrinking from threat, challenge, difficulty, or pain; speaking up for what's right even if there's opposition; acting on convictions even if unpopular; includes physical bravery but is not limited to it.

- **Perseverance** (persistence, industriousness): Finishing what one starts; persevering in a course of action in spite of obstacles; "getting it out the door"; taking pleasure in completing tasks.

- **Honesty** (authenticity, integrity): Speaking the truth but more broadly presenting oneself in a genuine way and acting in a sincere way; being without pretense; taking responsibility for one's feelings and actions.

- **Zest** (vitality, enthusiasm, vigor, energy): Approaching life with excitement and energy; not doing things halfway or halfheartedly; living life as an adventure; feeling alive and activated.

3. **Humanity:** Interpersonal strengths that involve tending and befriending others.

- **Love** (capacity to love and be loved): Valuing close relations with others, in particular those in which sharing and caring are reciprocated; being close to people.

- **Kindness** (generosity, nurturance, care, compassion, altruistic love, niceness): Doing favors and good deeds for others; helping them; taking care of them.

- **Social Intelligence** (emotional intelligence, personal intelligence): Being aware of the motives and feelings of others and oneself; knowing what to do to fit into different social situations; knowing what makes other people tick.

4. **Justice**: Civic strengths that underlie healthy community life.

   - **Teamwork** (citizenship, social responsibility, loyalty): Working well as a member of a group or team; being loyal to the group; doing one's share.

   - **Fairness**: Treating all people the same according to notions of fairness and justice; not letting feelings bias decisions about others; giving everyone a fair chance.

   - **Leadership**: Encouraging a group of which one is a member to get things done and at the same time maintain good relations within the group; organizing group activities and seeing that they happen.

5. **Temperance**: Strengths that protect against excess.

   - **Forgiveness** (mercy): Forgiving those who have done wrong; accepting others' shortcomings; giving people a second chance; not being vengeful.

   - **Humility** (modesty): Letting one's accomplishments speak for themselves; not regarding oneself as more special than one is.

○ **Prudence**: Being careful about one's choices; not taking undue risks; not saying or doing things that might later be regretted.

○ **Self-Regulation** (self-control): Regulating what one feels and does; being disciplined; controlling one's appetites and emotions.

6. **Transcendence**: Strengths that forge connections to the universe and provide meaning.

○ **Appreciation of Beauty and Excellence** (awe, wonder, elevation): Noticing and appreciating beauty, excellence, or skilled performance in various domains of life, from nature to art to mathematics to science to everyday experience.

○ **Gratitude**: Being aware of and thankful for the good things that happen; taking time to express thanks.

○ **Hope** (optimism, future-mindedness, future orientation): Expecting the best in the future and working to achieve it; believing that a good future is something that can be brought about.

○ **Humor** (playfulness): Liking to laugh and tease; bringing smiles to other people; seeing the light side; making (not necessarily telling) jokes.

○ **Spirituality** (religiousness, faith, purpose): Having coherent beliefs about the higher purpose and meaning of the universe; knowing where one fits within the larger scheme; having beliefs about the meaning of life that shape conduct and provide comfort.

# APPENDIX II: STUDY QUESTIONS FOR BOOK GROUPS

## INTRODUCTION

1. Reflect on a time when you were energized by your work. What factors were present that contributed to your energy?

2. Reflect on a time when your work felt draining. What factors were present that contributed to your fatigue?

3. Is your current work environment an example of a culture of control, a culture of indifference, or a connection culture? Why?

## CHAPTER 1

1. Describe a time when you truly connected with another person or a group. How did that make you feel?

2. Which of the six universal human needs to thrive at work are being met in your workplace? Which are not being sufficiently met?

3. What steps can you take to help meet the six universal needs for others in your workplace? Commit to taking two actions in the next week to meet others' needs (for example, affirm a colleague for a job well done).

## CHAPTER 2

1. Share an example of an organization that you believe shares a strong vision (inspiring identity).

- How is this vision communicated?

- Has the vision produced a shared identity that people connected with the organization feel proud about?

2. Share an example of an organization that you believe exhibits a strong sense of value (human value).

- How does the leadership show that it values employees?

- Has value in the organization produced a bond of shared empathy among people in the organization?

3. Share an example of an organization that you believe gives employees a strong voice.

- How does the organization encourage employees to provide feedback?

- Has voice in the organization resulted in a greater shared understanding?

4. Which of the 24 character strengths do you believe you exhibit? Which do you believe you need to strengthen?

## CHAPTER 3

1. Take a moment to reflect on the stories you read in this chapter. Which story did you find most inspiring? Why?

2. Write down three ideas you learned from the leaders highlighted in this chapter that you would like to implement in your own organization.

3. The common theme through each of the organizations featured in this chapter is a commitment to vision, value, and voice. How does your organization or team embody each of those elements? What elements need to be strengthened?

## CHAPTER 4

1. Research clearly shows that connection is critical for our personal health and well-being. On a scale of 1-10 (with 10 being fully connected), how would you rate your current level of personal connection?

2. Based on what you learned in this chapter about the importance of using connection to manage stress levels, write down two positive actions you can take the next time you feel overwhelmed at work. If you are a supervisor, write down two ways you can use connection to help your direct reports feel less stressed.

3. Organizations often display two or more of the three types of cultures. Which culture describes your team? Which cultures are present throughout the organization? If your team lacks a connection culture, consider contacting a leader in your organization who is an intentional connector and ask for tips on turning your team's culture around.

## CHAPTER 5

1. An important point made in this chapter is that connection occurs in subgroups, including across departments. Which departments or people are most critical for you to have strong relationships with? What is the current state of those relationships?

2. This chapter gives many practical tips for implementing a connection culture within your organization. Which three actions do you believe are most critical for your team at this point in time?

3. Connection is not just for the workplace. It's critical in all relationships, including community organizations, religious groups, families, and friends. What actions will you personally take to build connection in groups outside work?

## CHAPTER 6

1. What are your spheres of influence? How can you take steps to build connection in those local cultures?

2. Which of the three types of people (intentional disconnector, unintentional disconnector, or intentional connector) do you most frequently imitate?

3. Consider asking a few of those close to you to honestly share which of your habits or behaviors they find disconnecting. Doing so will help you to become aware of your connection blind spots.

# APPENDIX III:
# ADDITIONAL RESOURCES

To learn more about connection culture visit:

- *Connection Culture* website, www.connectionculture.com

- E Pluribus Partners' website, www.epluribuspartners.com

- Michael's blog, www.michaelleestallard.com

You can also subscribe to the Connect to Thrive email newsletter by visiting either the E Pluribus Partners' website or Michael's blog. When you subscribe, you will receive a welcome email that includes a free PDF copy of Michael's previous book, *Fired Up or Burned Out: How to Reignite Your Team's Passion, Creativity, and Productivity.*

# REFERENCES

## INTRODUCTION: THE SECRET OF U2'S SUCCESS

Assayas, M. 2005. *Bono: In Conversation with Michka Assayas*. New York: Penguin Group.

Bono, The Edge, A. Clayton, L. Mullen Jr., and N. McCormick. 2006. *U2 by U2*. New York: HarperCollins.

Clark, V. 2014. Telephone conversation with the author on April 4, 2014.

Gallup. 2013a. *State of the American Workplace: Employee Engagement Insights for U.S. Business Leaders*. Gallup. www.gallup.com /strategicconsulting/163007/state-american-workplace.aspx.

Gallup. 2013b. State of the Global Workplace: Employee Engagement Insights for Business Leaders Worldwide. Gallup. www.gallup.com /strategicconsulting/164735/state-global-workplace.aspx.

Garrett, G. 2009. *We Get to Carry Each Other: The Gospel According to U2*. Louisville, KY: Westminster John Knox Press.

Grammy.com. 2014. "U2: Past Grammy Awards." July 19. www.grammy.com /artist/u2.

Stevens, H. 2011. "Did U2 Just Surpass the Rolling Stones as the Greatest Band Ever?" *The Atlantic*, August 3. www.theatlantic.com/entertainment /archive/2011/08/did-u2-just-surpass-the-rolling-stones-as-the-greatest-band -ever/242943.

## CHAPTER 1: THE COMPETITIVE ADVANTAGE OF CONNECTION

Berkman, L., and L. Syme. 1979. "Social Networks, Host Resistance, and Mortality: A Nine-Year Study of Alameda County Residents." *American Journal of Epidemiology* 109(2): 186-204.

Corporate Leadership Council. 2004. *Driving Performance and Retention Through Employee Engagement*. Washington, DC: Corporate Executive Board.

Cromie, W.J. 1998. "Of Hugs and Hormones." *Harvard University Gazette*. June 11. www.news.harvard.edu/gazette/1998/06.11 /OfHugsandHormon.html.

Csikszentmihalyi, M. 1990. *Flow: The Psychology of Optimal Experience*. New York: Harper & Row.

Frankl, V. 1984. *Man's Search for Meaning: An Introduction to Logotherapy*. New York: Simon & Schuster.

Frederickson, B. 2003. "The Value of Positive Emotions." *American Scientist* 91(4): 330-335.

Gallup. 2013. *State of the American Workplace: Employee Engagement Insights for U.S. Business Leaders*. Gallup. www.gallup.com /strategicconsulting/163007/state-american-workplace.aspx.

Hallowell, E. 1999a. *Connect: 12 Vital Ties That Open Your Heart, Lengthen Your Life, and Deepen Your Soul*. New York: Pantheon.

Hallowell, E. 1999b. "The Human Moment at Work." *Harvard Business Review*, January, 58-66.

Harter, J., and F.L. Schmidt. 2010. "What Really Drives Financial Success." *Gallup Management Journal*, September. http://businessjournal.gallup.com /content/142733/really-drives-financial-success.aspx.

Institute for American Values. 2013. *Hardwired to Connect: The New Scientific Case for Authoritative Communities*. New York: Commission on Children at Risk. http://americanvalues.org/catalog/pdfs/hwexsumm.pdf.

Maslow, A.H. 1943. "A Theory of Human Motivation." *Psychological Review* 50:370-396.

Muir, D. 2014. "Meet Nick, a Hugger and Healer." *ABC News* video, April 24. www.youtube.com/watch?v=YX69Nn3DmfI.

Purvis, K., and D. Cross. 2012. TCU Institute of Child Development. www.child .tcu.edu.

Rowe, J., and R. Kahn. 1998. *Successful Aging*. New York: Pantheon.

Ryan, R., and E. Deci. 2001. "On Happiness and Human Potentials: A Review of Research on Hedonic and Eudaimonic Well-Being." *Annual Review of Psychology* 52:141-166.

Sapolsky, R. 2008. *Stress: Portrait of a Killer.* Documentary. National Geographic Television and Stanford University. http://killerstress .stanford.edu.

Schore, A. 2009. "Dr. Allan N. Schore." www.allanschore.com.

Stallard, M.L. 2007. *Fired Up or Burned Out: How to Reignite Your Team's Passion, Creativity, and Productivity.* Nashville, TN: Thomas Nelson.

Stallard, M.L. 2008. "The Connection Culture: A New Source of Competitive Advantage." *ChangeThis* 44(6). http://changethis.com/manifesto/44.06 .ConnectionCulture/pdf/44.06.ConnectionCulture.pdf.

Tronick, E. 2009. *Still Face Experiment: Dr. Edward Tronick.* November 30. www.youtube.com/watch?v=apzXGEbZht0.

Zaff, J.F., and K.A. Moore. 2002. "Promoting Well-Being Among America's Teens. John S. and James L. Knight Foundation." October. www.childtrends .org/wp-content/uploads/2002/10/Child_Trends-2002_10_01_ES _TeenWellbeing.pdf.

# CHAPTER 2: SHARED IDENTITY, EMPATHY, AND UNDERSTANDING

Burlingham, B. 1990. "This Woman Has Changed Business Forever." Inc.com, June 1. http://inc.com/magazine/19900601/5201.html.

Carney, B. 2005. "Toning Up The Body Shop." *Business Week*, May 18.

Hamel, G. 2012. *What Matters Now: How to Win in a World of Relentless Change, Ferocious Competition and Unstoppable Innovation.* San Francisco: Jossey-Bass, 193-205.

Hanessian, B., and C. Sierra. 2005. "Leading a Turnaround: An Interview with the Chairman of D&B." *McKinsey Quarterly*, May. www.mckinsey.com /insights/strategy/leading_a_turnaround_an _interview_with_the_chairman_of_d_and_b.

Hatfield, E., J.T. Cacioppo, and R.L. Rapson. 1994. *Emotional Contagion.* New York: Cambridge University Press.

Kearns Goodwin, D. 1994. *No Ordinary Time: Franklin and Eleanor Roosevelt: The Home Front in World War II.* New York: Simon & Schuster, 340.

Maruca, R.F., ed. 2006. *What Managers Say, What Employees Hear: Connecting with Your Front Line (So They'll Connect with Customers).* Westport, CT: Praeger, 131-132.

McCullough, D. 1991. *Brave Companions: Portraits in History*. New York: Prentice Hall Trade, xiv.

Peterson, C., and M.E.P. Seligman. 2004. *Character Strengths and Virtues: A Handbook and Classification*. New York: Oxford University Press; Washington, DC: American Psychological Association. www.viacharacter.org.

Stallard, M.L. 2007. *Fired Up or Burned Out: How to Reignite Your Team's Passion, Creativity, and Productivity*. Nashville, TN: Thomas Nelson.

The National WWII Museum. n.d. "By the Numbers: Wartime Production." The National WWII Museum. www.nationalww2museum.org/learn /education/for-students/ww2-history/ww2-by-the-numbers/wartime -production.html.

West, R. (Southwest Airline's Corporate Historian). 2014. Email to author dated June 11.

Wooden, J. 1997. *Wooden: A Lifetime of Observations and Reflections On and Off the Court*. New York: McGraw-Hill, 197.

# CHAPTER 3: CONNECTION: HIDDEN IN PLAIN SIGHT

Bartosek, N. 2011. "Why TCU Is the Hottest School in Texas." *Fort Worth Magazine,* July, 53-59.

Boschini, V. 2011. "Chancellor's Remarks: University Convocation and Founders' Celebration." September 8. www.chancellor.tcu.edu/speech -convocation-11.asp.

Bryant, A. 2011. "Google's Quest to Build a Better Boss." *New York Times,* March 12. www.nytimes.com/2011/03/13/business/13hire .html?pagewanted=all.

Byrne, J.A. 1990. "Profiting From the Nonprofits." *Business Week*, March 26. 66-74.

Chacko, P. 2011. "Trust quotient." Tata.com, May, www.tata.com /ourcommitment/articlesinside/v3fvyGw4b5Q=/TLYVr3YPkMU=.

Clark, V. 2002. "Presence, Power, Precision: The United States Navy in the 21st Century." *Sea Power*, April.

Clark, V. 2003. "Admiral Vern Clark Remarks." United States Naval Institute's 129th Annual Meeting & 13th Annapolis Seminar Luncheon at the Alumni Hall, United States Naval Academy, Annapolis, MD, April 3.

Deshpande, R. 2011. "The Ordinary Heroes of the Taj." *Harvard Business Review*, December, 119-123.

Elsdon-Dew, M. (Communications Director for Alpha International). 2014. Email to the author dated June 16.

Epstein, F., and J. Horwitz. 2003. *If I Get to Five: What Children Can Teach Us About Courage and Character*. New York: Henry Holt.

Google. 2009. Meetings with executives at Google's Googleplex headquarters in Mountain View, CA, on July 28.

Griffin, J. 2010. "The Lonely Society." The Mental Health Foundation. www .mentalhealth.org.uk/content/assets/PDF/publications/the_lonely_society _report.pdf?view=Standard.

Hadjian, A. 1995. "Follow the Leader." *Fortune*, November 27, 96.

Helgesen, S. 1995. *The Female Advantage: Women's Ways of Leadership*. New York: Doubleday.

Herdt, J., T. Lafluer, C.W. Moore Jr., F. Pandolfe, and F. Thorpe. 2008-2010. Personal meetings, telephone interviews, and emails to author about CNO Adm. Vern Clark and his leadership of the U.S. Navy. October 6, 2008, to June 10, 2010.

Hesselbein, F. 2002. *Hesselbein on Leadership*. San Francisco: Jossey-Bass.

Hoffman, B. 2012. "Nine Things I Learned from Alan Mulally." *Changethis*, April 11. http://changethis.com/manifesto/show/93.01.AmericanIcon.

Holy Trinity Brompton. 2011. HTB Leadership Conference and author's meetings with leaders of Alpha International and Holy Trinity Brompton from February 10 to 15.

McCann WorldGroup. 2011. "Truth About Youth." McCann World Group. http://truthcentral.mccann.com/truth-studies.

Mulally, A., and R. Kirkland. 2013. "Leading in the 21st Century: An Interview with Ford's Alan Mulally." McKinsey & Company Insights and Publications, November. www.mckinsey.com/insights/strategy/leading_in_the_21st_century _an_interview_with_fords _alan_mulally.

Osborne, R. 2012. "Victor Boschini." *Image* 43(Fall): 28-33.

Rajgopaul, R. 2010. "Salute to Ratan Tata." Ramana's Musings Blog. April 8. http://rummuser.com/?p=3182.

Sokolove, M. 2006. "Follow Me." *New York Times Magazine*, February 5. www.nytimes.com/2006/02/05/magazine/05coachk_96_101__116 _117_.html?pagewanted=all&_r=0.

Stallard, M.L. 2004. "7 Practices of Alan Mulally That Helped Ford Pass Competitors." Foxbusiness.com, January 22. www.foxbusiness.com /markets/2014/01/22/7-practices-alan-mulally-that-helped -ford-pass-competitors.

Stallard, M.L. 2007. *Fired Up or Burned Out: How to Reignite Your Team's Passion, Creativity, and Productivity*. Nashville, TN: Thomas Nelson.

Stallard, M.L., and J. Pankau. 2007. "Strengthening Human Value in Organizational Cultures." *Leader to Leader* 47:18-23.

StatSheet. 2014. "NCAA Basketball: Mike Krzyzewski." StatSheet. http://statsheet.com/mcb/coaches/mike-krzyzewski/career_record.

Stodghill, R. 2007. "The Doctor Is In." *New York Times*, January 7. www.nytimes.com/2007/01/07/business/yourmoney/07hospital.html ?pagewanted=all.

Tata Group. 2014. *The Tata Way*. Internal Publication.

Texas Christian University. Meetings, emails, and telephone calls the author had with TCU administrators, faculty, and students from 2010 to 2014.

U.S. Navy. 2009. "Top Five Priorities, Articles, Speeches, Interviews, etc. of Admiral Vern Clark, Chief of Naval Operations, USN." U.S. Department of the Navy, August 1. www.navy.mil/navydata/nav_legacy.asp?id=215.

Vlasic, B. 2014. "Complete U-Turn: The Head of Ford Retires, Having Rejuvenated the Carmaker." *New York Times*, May 1. www.nytimes .com/2014/05/02/business/ford-motor-chief-to-retire.html?_r=0.

# CHAPTER 4: THE SCIENTIFIC CASE FOR CONNECTION

Ackerlind, I., and J.O. Hornquist. 1992. "Loneliness and Alcohol Abuse: A Review of Evidence of an Interplay." *Social Science and Medicine* 34:405-414.

Anderson, G. 2010. "Loneliness Among Older Adults: A National Survey of Adults 45+." *AARP*, September. www.aarp.org/personal-growth/transitions /info-09-2010/loneliness_2010.html.

Baumeister, R.F., C.N. DeWall, N.J. Ciarocco, and J.M. Twenge. 2005. "Social Exclusion Impairs Self-Regulation." *Journal of Personality and Social Psychology* 88:589-604.

Baumeister, R.F., J.M. Twenge, and C.K. Nuss. 2002. "Effects of Social Exclusion on Cognitive Processes: Anticipated Aloneness Reduces Intelligent Thought." *Journal of Personality and Social Psychology* 83:817-827.

Berkman, L., and L. Syme. 1979. "Social Networks, Host Resistance and Mortality: A Nine-Year Study of Alameda County Residents." *American Journal of Epidemiology* 109(2): 186-204.

Brooks, D. 2011. *The Social Animal: The Hidden Sources of Love, Character and Achievement*. New York: Random House.

Bruhn, J.G., and S. Wolf. 1979. *The Roseto Story*. Norman: University of Oklahoma Press.

Bryant, A. 2011. "Google's Quest to Build a Better Boss." *New York Times*, March 12. www.nytimes.com/2011/03/13/business/13hire .html?pagewanted=all.

Cacioppo, J., and W. Patrick. 2008. *Loneliness: Human Nature and the Need for Social Connection*. New York: W.W. Norton & Company.

CASA (The National Center on Addiction and Substance Abuse at Columbia University). 2007. "Illegal Drug Use Up from 1992 Lows; Americans, 4 Percent of the World Population, Consume Two-Thirds of World's Illegal Drugs." Market Wired, May 7. www.marketwired.com/press-release /califano-calls-fundamental-shift-attitudes-policies-about-substance-abuse -addiction-731322.htm.

CDC (Centers for Disease Control & Prevention). 2012. "An Estimated 1 in 10 U.S. Adults Report Depression." CDC, April 20. www.cdc.gov/features /dsdepression

Census of Housing. 2011. "Historical Census of Housing Tables." U.S. Census Bureau, October 31. www.census.gov/hhes/www/housing/census/historic /livalone.html.

Coric, D., and B.I. Murstein. 1993. "Eating Disorders." *The Journal of Treatment & Prevention* 1(1): 39-51.

Corporate Leadership Council. 2004. *Driving Performance and Retention Through Employee Engagement*. Washington, DC: Corporate Executive Board.

de Geus, A. 1997. "The Living Company." *Harvard Business Review*, March-April, 51-59.

Ferrie, J., ed. 2004. "Work Stress and Health: the Whitehall II Study." London: Public and Commercial Services Union. www.ucl.ac.uk/whitehallII/pdf /Whitehallbooklet_1_.pdf.

Fleming, J.H., C. Coffman, and J.K. Harter. 2005. "Manage Your Human Sigma." *Harvard Business Review*, July-August.

Gallup. 2013a. *State of the American Workplace: Employee Engagement Insights for U.S. Business Leaders*. www.gallup.com /strategicconsulting/163007/state-american-workplace.aspx.

Gallup. 2013b. *Engagement at Work: Effect on Performance Continues in Tough Economic Times—Key Findings from Gallup's Q12 Meta-Analysis of 1.4 Million Employees*. www.gallup.com/strategicconsulting/161459 /engagement-work-effect-performance-continues-tough-economic-times.aspx.

Gibbons, J. 2007. "Finding a Definition of Employee Engagement." The Conference Board Executive Action Series, June.

Gladwell, M. 2008. *Outliers: The Story of Success*. New York: Little, Brown, 3-11.

Goldsmith, S.K., T.C. Pellmar, A.M. Kleinman, and W.E. Bunny. 2002. *Reducing Suicide: A National Imperative*. Washington, DC: National Academy Press.

Goleman, D. 2006. *Social Intelligence: The New Science of Human Relationships*. New York: Random House, 147-156.

Hallowell, E. 1999. *Connect: 12 Vital Ties That Open Your Heart, Lengthen Your Life, and Deepen Your Soul*. New York: Pantheon.

Harter, J.K., F.L. Schmidt, J.W. Asplund, E. A. Killham, and S. Agrawal. 2010. "Causal Impact of Employee Work Perceptions on the Bottom Line of Organizations." Perspectives on Psychological Science 5(4): 378-389.

Hay Group. 2010. "Creating High Performing Organizations: Being an Employer of Choice." Hay Group. www.haygroup.com/downloads/id/misc /hay_group_article_creating_high_performing_org_-_eoc_2010-oct1.pdf.

Heath, C., and D. Heath. 2010. *Made to Stick: How to Change Things When Change is Hard*. New York: Crown.

Hewitt Associates. 2004. "Research Brief: Employee Engagement Higher at Double-Digit Growth Companies." Hewitt Associates, May. www.mckpeople.com.au/SiteMedia/w3svc161/Uploads/Documents/016fc140-895a-41bf-90df-9ddb28f4bdab.pdf.

Hurley, D. 2013. "Grandma's Experiences Leave a Mark on Your Genes." *Discover*, June 11. http://discovermagazine.com/2013/may/13-grandmas-experiences-leave-epigenetic-mark-on-your-genes.

Karen, R. 1990. "Becoming Attached." *The Atlantic*, February. www.theatlantic.com/magazine/archive/1990/02/becoming-attached/308966.

Kaufman, J., R. Markey, S. Dey Burton, and D. Azzarello. 2013. "Who's Responsible for Employee Engagement?" Bain & Company, December 11. www.bain.com/publications/articles/whos-responsible-for-employee-engagement.aspx.

Lieberman, M. 2013. *Social: Why Our Brains Are Wired to Connect*. New York: Crown.

Marche, S. 2012. "Is Facebook Making Us Lonely?" *The Atlantic*, April. www.theatlantic.com/magazine/archive/2012/05/is-facebook-making-us-lonely/308930.

Martin, R. 2007. *The Opposable Mind: How Successful Leaders Win Through Integrative Thinking*. Boston: Harvard Business School Publishing.

McCann WorldGroup. 2011. "Truth About Youth." McCann WorldGroup. http://truthcentral.mccann.com/ truth-studies.

Morris, J. 2014. Correspondence to author, June 14.

Olds, J., and R. Schwartz. 2009. *The Lonely American: Drifting Apart in the Twenty-First Century*. Boston: Beacon Press, 72-73.

Rath, T., and J. Harter. 2010. *Well Being: The Five Essential Elements*. New York: Gallup Press, 39, 41, 103.

Rocket, I.R.H., M.D. Regier, N.D. Kapusta, J.H. Coben, T.R. Miller, R.L. Hanzlick, K.H. Todd, R.W. Sattin, L.W. Kennedy, J. Kleinig, and G.S. Smith. 2012. "Leading Causes of Unintentional and Intentional Injury Mortality: United States, 2000-2009." American Journal of Public Health 102(11): e84-e92. http://ajph.aphapublications.org/doi/full/10.2105/AJPH.2012.300960.

Rowe, J.W., and R.L. Kahn. 1998. *Successful Aging.* New York: Pantheon, 152-156.

Sapolsky, R. 2008. *Stress: Portrait of a Killer.* Documentary. National Geographic Television and Stanford University. http://killerstress.stanford.edu.

Sapolsky, R. 2010. *Stress and Your Body.* Chantilly, VA: The Teaching Company.

Schaef, A.W. 1987. *When Society Becomes an Addict.* New York: Harper Collins.

Sherman, G.D., J.J. Lee, A.J.C. Cuddy, J. Renshon's, C. Oveis, J.J. Gross, and J.S. Lerner. 2012. "Leadership Is Associated with Lower Levels of Stress." *Proceedings of the National Academy of Sciences of the United States of America* 109(44): 17903-17907.

Shirom, A., S. Toker, Y. Alkaly, O. Jacobson, and R. Balicer. 2011. "Worked-Based Predictors of Mortality: A 20-Year Follow-Up of Healthy Employees." *Health Psychology* 30(3): 268-275.

Stacy, A.W., M.D. Newcomb, and P.M. Bentler. 1995. "Expectancy in Mediational Models of Cocaine Abuse." *Personality and Individual Differences* 19(5): 655-667.

Stallard, M.L. 2007. *Fired Up or Burned Out: How to Reignite Your Team's Passion, Creativity, and Productivity.* Nashville, TN: Thomas Nelson.

Sussman, S., N. Lisha, and M. Griffiths. 2011. "Prevalence of the Addictions: A Problem of the Majority or the Minority?" *Evaluation & the Health Professions* 34(1): 3-56.

Temkin Group. 2013. "Employee Engagement Benchmark Study 2013." Temkin Group Research, January. www.temkingroup.com/research-reports/employee-engagement-benchmark-study-2013.

Twenge, J.M., R.F. Baumeister, D.M. Tice, and T.S. Stucke. 2001. "If You Can't Join Them, Beat Them: Effects of Social Exclusion on Aggressive Behavior." *Journal of Personality and Social Psychology* 81:1058-1069.

Twenge, J.M., K.R. Catanes, and R.F. Baumeister. 2002. "Social Exclusion Causes Self-Defeating Behavior." *Journal of Personality and Social Psychology* 83:606-615.

Valliant, G.E. 2012. *Triumphs of Experience: The Men of the Harvard Grant Study.* Cambridge, MA: Belknap Press of Harvard University Press.

Vespa, J., J.M. Lewis, and R.M. Kreider. 2013. "America's Families Living Arrangements: 2012." United States Census Bureau, August. www.census.gov /prod/2013pubs/p20-570.pdf.

Wilson, E.O. 2012. *The Social Conquest of Earth*. New York: Liveright.

Woolf, S.H., and L. Aron, eds. 2014. *U.S. Health in International Perspective: Shorter Lives, Poorer Health*. Washington, DC: The National Academies Press.

## CHAPTER 5: TAKING ACTION: CONNECTING THROUGH VISION, VALUE, AND VOICE

Behar, H. 2007. *It's Not About the Coffee: Leadership Principles from a Life at Starbucks*. New York: Portfolio, 94-96.

Behar, H. 2009. "Starbucks: It's Not About the Coffee." Interview by M.L. Stallard. BrightTalk, March 27. www.brighttalk.com/webcast/89/2408.

Chapman, G., and P. White. 2011. *The 5 Languages of Appreciation in the Workplace: Empowering Organizations by Encouraging People*. Chicago: Northfield Publishing.

Derrick, S., and K. Wooley. 2009. Meetings with Scott Derrick and Kitty Wooley of 13L.

Dorsey, D. 2000. "Positive Deviant." *Fast Company*, November 30. www.fastcompany.com/42075/positive-deviant.

Dutton, J. 2003. *Energize Your Workplace: How to Create and Sustain High Quality Connections at Work*. San Francisco: Jossey-Bass, 39.

Flash Mentoring. n.d. "What Is Flash Mentoring?" www.flashmentoring.com.

Fredrickson, B. 2009. *Positivity: Top-Notch Research Reveals 3-to-1 Ratio That Will Change Your Life*. New York: Three Rivers Press.

Fredrickson, B. 2013. "Your Phone vs. Your Heart." *New York Times*, March 24. www.nytimes.com/2013/03/24/opinion/sunday/your-phone-vs-your -heart.html

Fredrickson, B., K.M. Grewen, K.A. Coffey, S.B. Algoe, A.M. Firestine, J.M.G. Arevalo, J. Ma, and S.W. Cole. 2013. "A Functional Genomic Perspective on Human Well-Being." *Proceedings of the National Academy of Sciences* 110(33): 13684-13689.

Fredrickson, B., and T. Joiner. 2002. "Positive Emotions Trigger Upward Spirals Toward Emotional Well-Being." *Psychological Science* 13(2). www.unc.edu /peplab/_publications/Fredrickson _Joiner_2002.pdf.

Goldsmith, M. *What Got You Here Won't Get You There: How Successful People Become Even More Successful!* New York: Hyperion.

Goleman, D. 2006. *Social Intelligence: The New Science of Human Relationships.* New York: Random House.

Google. 2009. Meetings with executives at Google's Googleplex headquarters in Mountain View, CA, on July 28.

Gottman, J. 1994. *Why Marriages Succeed or Fail.* New York: Simon and Schuster.

Hsieh, T. 2010. Conversation with Tony Hsieh, Zappo's CEO, in a meeting with the author on September 15.

Morris, J. 2014. Meeting and correspondence with author.

Pennebaker, J. 1997. *Opening Up: The Healing Power of Expressing Emotions.* New York: Guilford Press.

Pfeffer, J., and R. Sutton. 2000. *The Knowing-Doing Gap: How Smart Companies Turn Knowledge Into Action.* Cambridge, MA: Belknap Press of Harvard University Press.

Soames, M. 1999. *Speaking for Themselves: The Private Letters of Sir Winston and Lady Churchill.* Black Swan. Quoted in Lee, N., and S. Lee. 2000. *The Marriage Book.* London: Alpha International.

Spiegelman, P. 2012. *Smile Guide: Employee Perspectives on Culture, Loyalty, and Profit.* Dallas: Brown Books.

Stallard, M.L. 2007. *Fired Up or Burned Out: How to Reignite Your Team's Passion, Creativity, and Productivity.* Nashville, TN: Thomas Nelson.

Stallard, M.L. 2010. "Has Jim Goodnight Cracked the Code on Corporate Culture?" Michael Lee Stallard Blog, June 18. www.michaelleestallard.com /has-jim-goodnight-cracked-the-code-of-corporate-culture.

# CHAPTER 6: WHOM WILL YOU CHOOSE TO BECOME?

Catmull, E. 2008. "How Pixar Fosters Collective Creativity." *Harvard Business Review*, September.

Catmull, E. 2014. *Creativity, Inc.: Overcoming the Unseen Forces That Stand in the Way of True Inspiration*. New York: Random House.

Goleman, D. 2006. *Social Intelligence: The New Science of Human Relationships*. New York: Random House, 117-132.

Stallard, M. 2009. "The Incredibles: Ed Catmull." *Economic Times*, June 5.

Walker, J. 2008. Meeting with author in April.

Zimbardo, P. 2007. *The Lucifer Effect: Understanding How Good People Turn Evil*. New York: Random House.

Zimbardo, P. 2008. "The Psychology of Evil." TED2008, February. www.ted.com/talks/philip_zimbardo_on_the_psychology_of_evil.

# ABOUT THE AUTHOR
# AND CONTRIBUTORS

## MICHAEL LEE STALLARD

Michael is co-founder and president of E Pluribus Partners. He speaks, teaches, coaches, and consults for a wide variety of organizations including Foote, Cone & Belding, General Electric, Google, Johnson & Johnson, Lockheed Martin, MD Anderson Cancer Center, NASA, Texas Christian University, U.S. Department of Treasury, and Yale New Haven Health System. He is the primary author of *Fired Up or Burned Out: How to Reignite Your Team's Passion, Creativity, and Productivity*, and a contributor to several books, including *What Managers Say, What Employees Hear: Connecting With Your Front Line (So They'll Connect With Customers)*, and the *ASTD Management Development Handbook*.

Articles written by Michael or about his work have appeared in the *Wall Street Journal*, the *New York Times*, *Leader to Leader*, *HR Magazine*, *Human Resource Executive*, *Leadership Excellence*, *Fox Business Now*, *Training Industry Quarterly*, *Capital* (Dubai), *Rotman* (Canada), *The Economic Times* (India), *Developing HR Strategy* (UK), *Shukan Diayamondo* (Japan), and *Outlook Business for Decision Makers* (India). He has spoken at conferences organized by the Conference Board, the Corporate Executive Board, the Human Capital Institute, *Fortune* magazine, the Innovation Council, and the World Presidents Organization. He is a faculty member of the Institute for Management Studies (IMS), and he has been a guest lecturer at many universities including the University of Virginia's Darden Graduate School of Business, Texas Christian University, and University of Toronto's Rotman School of Management.

Prior to founding E Pluribus Partners, Michael was chief marketing officer for businesses at Morgan Stanley and Charles Schwab. The programs his team identified and implemented at Morgan Stanley contributed to doubling a business unit's revenues during a two-and-a-half year period. The practices he and his team developed became the genesis for his approach to elevating the productivity and innovation of individuals and organizations. Michael has also worked as an executive in marketing and finance positions at Texas Instruments, Van Kampen Investments, and Barclays Bank, PLC. He received a BS in marketing from Illinois State University, an MBA from the University of Texas Permian Basin, and a JD from DePaul University Law School. He was admitted to the Illinois bar in 1991. Michael is married and has two daughters.

## JASON PANKAU

Jason is a co-founder and partner at E Pluribus Partners. He speaks, teaches, coaches, and consults for the firm's clients. Jason guest lectured at the University of Virginia's Darden Graduate School of Business, and has spoken or taught seminars at a wide variety of organizations, including Arkansas Electric, General Dynamics, Gen Re, Johnson & Johnson, the MD Anderson Cancer Center, NASA, and Scotiabank. He wrote the book *Beyond Self Help*, contributed to *Fired Up or Burned Out: How to Reignite Your Team's Passion, Creativity, and Productivity* and *What Managers Say, What Employees Hear: Connecting With Your Front Line (So They'll Connect With Customers)*, and has also written articles for *Leader to Leader* and *Leadership Excellence*.

Jason is also the president of Life Spring Network, a Christian organization that trains and coaches pastors and church leaders. He teaches seminars on leadership, marriage, and discipleship throughout North America, and has started churches and served as a pastor focused on mentoring and leadership development.

Jason earned a BS from Brown University in business economics and organizational behavior/management. While there, he was captain and pre-season All-American linebacker in football, school record holder in discus, and national qualifier in track. Jason earned a master's of divinity from Southern Theological Seminary, and has completed the required coursework for a doctorate in leadership at Gordon-Conwell Theological Seminary. Jason is married and has two daughters and two sons.

## KATHARINE P. STALLARD

Katie is a partner at E Pluribus Partners. She is a gifted connector, speaker, and teacher who brings diverse experience in marketing, administration, business, and nonprofit organizations to her role. Audiences and seminar participants enjoy her sense of humor and practical advice. Katie has worked in marketing for Tyndale House Publishers, a leading global Christian book publisher; for a Forbes 400 family helping to manage their diverse holdings; and currently leads communications for a highly regarded church in Greenwich, Connecticut. She also has extensive experience helping and serving on the boards of education and social sector organizations. Katie graduated cum laude from the University of Illinois with a BS in business administration.

# INDEX

# HOW TO PURCHASE ATD PRESS PUBLICATIONS

ATD Press publications are available worldwide in print and electronic format.

To place an order, please visit our online store: www.td.org/books.

Our publications are also available at select online and brick-and-mortar retailers.

Outside the United States, English-language ATD Press titles may be purchased through the following distributors:

**United Kingdom, Continental Europe, the Middle East, North Africa, Central Asia, Australia, New Zealand, and Latin America**
Eurospan Group
Phone: 44.1767.604.972
Fax: 44.1767.601.640
Email: eurospan@turpin-distribution.com
Website: www.eurospanbookstore.com

**Asia**
Cengage Learning Asia Pte. Ltd.
Phone: (65)6410-1200
Email: asia.info@cengage.com
Website: www.cengageasia.com

**Nigeria**
Paradise Bookshops
Phone: 08033075133
Email: paradisebookshops@gmail.com
Website: www.paradisebookshops.com

**South Africa**
Knowledge Resources
Phone: +27 (11) 706.6009
Fax: +27 (11) 706.1127
Email: sharon@knowres.co.za
Web: www.kr.co.za

For all other territories, customers may place their orders at the ATD online store: **www.td.org/books**.

0215145.62220